A HYPNOTIST'S JOURNEY
TO ATLANTIS

SARAH BRESKMAN COSME

ACKNOWLEDGMENTS

Thank you to all my friends and family for your love and support.

Thank you to Dr. Brian Weiss, Dolores Cannon, and Julia Cannon
for sharing your teachings with me.

Thank you to all the QHHT practitioners all over the world and those who support them.

And finally, thank you to all the clients who allowed me to share their stories in this book, and especially, with deep gratitude from the bottom of my heart, I thank Jen, who, without her sacrifice, none of this would be writte

CONTENTS

"The information about Atlantis and Lymuria has been buried for thousands and thousands of years because the information is so powerful it would create change amongst the people."

-The Subconscious

INTRODUCTION

I never thought to write a book like this. It just seemed to fall into my life, just as I am sure it has in previous lifetimes. Through my work in past life regression hypnosis I have learned that I have written this story before; yet the remnants of it are forever lost under the shifting sands of time. Once again, it has found its way to me and unrelentingly begs to be told. The information I was given has shown up in my life as unsolicited gifts that have been pulled together by the great forces of our universe. I have learned through the course of writing this book that there truly are no coincidences in life, that there is a force that pulls us inexorably toward what we require. In my work, I believe I have uncovered a piece of forgotten history, a moment in time that stands decisively for humankind, but has been erased from our minds for our own protection. I believe this story needs to be told as it has a strong correlation with what is going on in the topsy-turvy world we now find around us. I know it is time to bring this information back and allow those who relate to it to find peace amidst their confusion. With the desire to share what I have found (an alternate version of our humble beginnings on this planet), I write this book with the same dedication and fervor as I once did.

As a society we have all been curious when it comes to the subject of Atlantis and Lymuria. Legends have been told for generations, and famous writers like Plato and Edgar Cayce have foretold tales of their splendor and greatness. In my work as a practitioner of past life regression hypnosis, people often ask about the questionability of the continent's existences and their missing locations from the maps of time. I have often wondered why so many people claim to have strange memories or dreams about these places. If you have ever wondered yourself, or are curious, you have come to the right book; or more likely, this book has found its way to you. Undoubtedly, there is a great awakening happening around us right now. Humans have existed for thousands of years with a clouded understanding of how our reality works and how society works within that. There is a great need to overthrow the oppression that has molded us for so long. It is time for us to look with fresh eyes at the story of our origin and see our true selves for what we are and learn of the deep connections that unite us all. Reader, be prepared to be triggered, awakened, and even to recall your own experience during this catastrophic time in forgotten history.

My Journey

My journey into this work started with a curiosity mixed with a deep desire to help others heal themselves. Suffering from many childhood issues (being overweight, nervousness, OCD, and sleep issues) I had gone to traditional therapy for much of my young adult life and even though this was a blessing, I did not find the results I desired. It was not until I went off to college and returned home two months later that I noticed something very different about myself and the issues that had plagued me for years. Entering back into my parent's house I walked by a mirror and noticed something. While I was away for those two months, I had lost weight, forgotten to have obsessive compulsive disorder, calmed my anxiety and had even been able to sleep. It struck me as strange, as I had tried on many occasions to release these habits, especially in therapy, and yet, all of a sudden, I felt cured. I realized in that moment that there was a strong link between my recovery and the change of environment I had undertaken. It was a new concept to digest, but I realized that changing my environment had caused me to change my thoughts which had, in turn, changed my life! This was something new to me and yet still I pushed this aside and finished my degree as I did not see a need to expand on this concept at the time. As I have learned, life has a way of pulling things into your path so that you may experience things in their due time.

It was no surprise that the journey of my life and everything in it led me to past life regression work. Dr. Brian Weiss, author of *Many Lives, Many Masters,* was my first teacher. With such a calm demeanor and captivating personality, he delivered such profound ideas and lessons that truly changed the trajectory of my life. Dr. Brian Weiss started his career as a traditional psychotherapist until one of his patients began recalling past-life traumas that seemed to hold the key to her recurring nightmares and anxiety attacks. As a once proclaimed skeptic he was astonished as she began to channel messages from the space between lives. Using this new method of past-life therapy he was able to cure the patient and embark on this new career.

Years later I discovered Dolores Cannon's work, *Quantum Healing Hypnosis Technique.* From the moment I stumbled upon her work, I knew I was meant to do it. Dolores Cannon was an American hypnotist and self-published author of 17 non-fiction books mostly composed of transcripts from past life regression sessions. Cannon's innovative QHHT Technique allows me to delve into the future, the past, and current events through asking my clients' all-knowing, all-loving, and powerful subconscious. I delved into practicing her method and spent a few years moving up from a level 1 to a level 3 practitioner. Currently, I am one of only 14 people in the world who have this qualification, and I spread the knowledge as an educator internationally.

The information found in this book was found through hypnosis techniques learned from Dr. Brian Weiss, Dolores Cannon, and her daughter Julia Cannon. In order to increase the validity of the information, I have used multiple clients who have never met and do not have any previous knowledge of Lymuria or Atlantis. The information was not researched. All of it comes from actual memories recalled during hypnosis.

What is QHHT?

In a QHHT session the client is guided through a past life or lives in order to get the client deep enough into hypnosis. This is in order to gain a clear access to the subconscious. Known by many names, the subconscious has been called by various names such as the Superconscious, the Over Soul, God, and Source, among others. However, Dolores Cannon decided that she would just call it the Subconscious when dealing with it to make it easier, so that is what I do. Throughout this book, this is the hypnosis technique that I used for the most part. In some cases, and in earlier sessions that I am including, I also used the past life regression technique taught to me by Dr. Brian Weiss.

What is Atlantis?

From the many hypnosis sessions I have performed, I have learned from my clients that Atlantis was an island located in the Atlantic Ocean, and that it stretched from Europe to America and over to Africa near Egypt. It extended from the top portion of Western Africa to as far north as North Carolina and Virginia. Many clients have noticed the globe looked different in its land mass shape than it does now, with water and coastlines in altered locations. North Africa was seen as a lone sandbar in a sea that extended from the Great Sphinx of Egypt to Atlantis. Atlantis was not a tropical island. The weather was cooler and pine trees were found abundantly along the rocky island perimeter. Clients have commented on tall pine trees that grew out of grey cube-like boulders lining most of the coast of Atlantis. There was a high level of male domination in their hierarchy and government structure, and that bias would trickle down into their sciences and discoveries. Atlantis was foremost a society of scientists who valued technology, innovations and inventions. If you look at what is the true essence of Atlantis, it is the fractioning off from the female power that began the path into the male domination we see around us today.

Chapter 1. THE BEGINNING

I met Jen in 2008, before I had even begun to practice as a hypnotist. As I've learned now, there really are no coincidences. As if set up by the universe to eventually work together, we lived in the same small town, had children of similar ages who went to the same school, and thus, often attended the same social engagements. And if that wasn't enough, we both had a third child later on in life at about the same time, which led us to start talking after school as we watched our children on the playground.

It was 2009, and at the time I was just beginning to navigate my way into the world of hypnosis, working first with clients who needed help with smoking cessation, weight loss, and other habitual problems related to overall health and wellbeing. Throughout the many years I had known Jen, she had often voiced a desire to lose weight, so I felt she was a perfect candidate for my studies. As I had predicted, Jen happily volunteered to undergo these sessions with me, and was as excited as I was to begin. However, after a total of three weight loss hypnosis sessions, Jen's weight did not budge. There was something blocking her weight loss, and we both knew it.

In 2018, after years of delving into Dolores Cannon's QHHT, I needed to find a subject who was willing to be recorded while under hypnosis. This was a requirement to attain the coveted Level Three certification, a certification that signifies the mastering of her practice. For some unknown reason, my first instinct was to ask Jen if she was interested in helping me. I still do not know why I asked her that day, but as I look back on it now, this was obviously divinely planned.

As a practitioner of QHHT and past life regression hypnosis, I made it a habit of never being first to approach the subject of spirituality with my clients. In fact, I felt it was important for my clients to bring up this topic on their own, and with Jen, it was the same. We had never discussed our beliefs, even in our casual meetings as friends. In addition to this, we had also never discussed our beliefs regarding our existence on this earth, or the history from which we truly descended. In fact, I specifically felt Jen was an ideal subject because she had no knowledge of Dolores Cannon or past life regression hypnosis.

"I have been looking for something exactly like what you are talking about," Jen said when I asked if she would be my subject. I explained to her that this method was a deep journey inwards, in which she could expect to connect with her innermost self. I explained that in our session she would be able to find out more information about who she really was, and perhaps delve into her true purpose, explore past lives, and all the while, use this information to heal her body.

"I have been searching for something like this," she said, "because I've just been diagnosed with a brain condition called Pseudo Tumor Cerebri." Jen explained that this was similar to a brain tumor except her tumor was filled with water. She explained that it caused a lack of vision, lethargy and extreme headaches from the fluid suffocating her brain. The only treatment known for this type of illness was a treatment involving heavy doses of pharmaceuticals, and even with those the prognosis was a grim one. After listening to Jen, instead of panic or sadness in that moment, I actually felt excitement for her because I knew I could help. I have always felt at my core an inexplicable knowing that I possess some sort of innate healing ability. Perhaps this is what all healers feel at their core; a knowledge that comes from lifetimes and lifetimes of doing healing work. Although I knew that as a QHHT practitioner, I wasn't the one who would be doing the healing, but simply facilitating the process. Jen would have to heal her brain condition on her own terms, and my training was the answer she had been looking for, perhaps without even knowing. Somehow, I knew in that first discussion that I could help Jen help herself. I knew intuitively that it would be done, and after our first session, it was.

Our first session led to results that weren't just remarkable, they were nearly unexplainable, especially to the medical specialists who had diagnosed and were treating her. They were baffled by how the cerebral fluid that had once been suffocating her brain for months had suddenly leveled out, all without any pharmaceutical medications.

What follows is our first session, perhaps the first session that solidified my career path further into QHHT. At the time, even as a student in February of 2018, I still had little understanding of Atlantis and Lymuria. I was in no means an expert on these ancient civilizations, but little did I know, that was all about to change. It is clear to me now that the universe plotted to bring us together to get this information out and into the world; information so powerful that it could heal the swelling in Jen's brain. There is an actual activation of energy that can be felt when listening to the original following transcript of our first session, and so that none of it is lost, I have transcribed it here as it unfolded.

As taught by Dolores and as part of the QHHT method, I directed Jen to "float down" into her surroundings and describe what she saw.

Sarah: What do you become aware of?
Jen: I recognize what I see, it looks like NYC from above at night. It's a lot slower than I think it would be, it feels like it's in the 70's.
S: Do you see any modes of transportation?
J: Yes, the cars, they look boxier. Everything just looks less overpopulated. It's still very vibrant, I see the orange and red lights.
S: Do you get a sense of what you're doing there?
J: I think I'm just watching the activity.
S: Is there anything interesting about what you see?
J: The bridges, and the lights on these bridges. The way they're blinking; it's like they're warning.
S: What type of warning are they giving?
J: To not fly into them.
S: Do you get a sense of what you're doing up there?

J: It's a way to stick around and watch people.

S: *Do you want to stay up there, or do you come down to the bottom?*

J: It's hard to go to the bottom because people may see me and it's safer to stay up above. It's a different perspective up above.

S: *How would you describe yourself there?*

J: I don't think I'm alive. I am like a mist, a loose outline of a human body. Like a vapor almost.

S: *Do you get a sense of what you're doing there?*

J: I feel like I'm looking for someone. I'm watching for someone; I'm supposed to help them.

S: *Who?*

J: A young girl who will be lured into the park.

S: *What are you doing for her?*

J: She is not ready to go but has been very misguided.

S: *By who?*

J: Her parents are massive drug addicts. If she goes into the park she will be killed, defiled, but she must live.

S: *Why must she live?*

J: She has a mission. And she must complete it. Her mission is a medical mission. It is a breakthrough. It will be an area of disease control, and it will allow people to prolong their lives with certain diseases where there was no expectancy before. I believe it has something to do with AIDs or HIV.

S: *Is this something she carries within her?*

J: Her experiences will allow her to relate to this field and her environment. They will show her the need for such a medical mission that will give life back to people as her life will be given back to her. She's supposed to help find a cure, well not exactly a cure, but a way to prolong life and give people who have been affected by these diseases a new lease on life.

S: *What type of help is she going to provide?*

J: She will provide the theory that leads to the drug and this medical breakthrough that will happen.

S: *And why are you assigned to help her?*

J: I had requested to stay in the area, and it was my assignment.

S: *Did you choose this assignment or was it chosen for you?*

J: The assignment was less a choice and more of a match between the two. There is no word for what it is. There is no powerful enough word in this language to describe our soul contracts.

S: *Did you plan with this girl to be the one to help her?*

J: I believe she understood the contract as I understood it, but the contract is not as necessary when you are in between [lives]. And if it's a specific job, the other person will have the other end of the contract.

S: *Ok, well if this was her plan to be so instrumental, why would she go into the park in the first place?*

J: She's scared of her parents, they're some of the first crack addicts of the New York City epidemic, and they will harm her. She has run from harm into harm, and she has no protection.

S: *Did she plan to have crack addict parents?*

J: Yes.

S: *Was it part of the plan to go into Central Park?*

J: It was driven by fear and looks well designed as if this experience will shape the need to bring life back to people who have been issued a death warrant. It will be instrumental in her vibrational access to this information to have that feeling of being given back her life.

S: *What if she had gone into the park? What would've happened?*

J: She would've been terribly raped and murdered by a group of four homeless drug addicts under an overpass, a small bridge overpass.

S: *Then she wouldn't have fulfilled her mission. How do you stop this? How do you intervene?*

J: I find her, and I see her. She's sitting on a bench trying to sleep, and it's very loud and the streetlights are flashing red and green and yellow and keeping her awake. Instead of letting her go into the park to find a place to sleep, I put her to sleep.

S: *How?*

J: I lay my hands on either side of the head and I focus this energy which puts her to sleep. But as she dreams, she knows that I'm there.

S: *How?*

J: She can feel me. She's very aware in her dream of what's going on.

S: *Tell me more.*

J: She believes her purpose now.

S: *When she wakes up, does she remember this consciously?*

J: Yes.

S: *What kind of meaning did this have for you?*

J: I knew what she would accomplish and what it would mean for people, and that was the determining factor and the drive for this. Not all people should be saved, but some do need to be saved. Especially when they cannot help themselves.

S: *How does this feel?*

J: It was destined all along. I felt a sense of warmth in my heart, as if I were protecting one of my children. Similar but different.

S: *Can anyone call on you?*

J: No, the situation must be a match between the rescuer and the rescued. It must be a predestined match, a path to unfold that is best for all involved and for the continuation of all that we see. If it is not, then it needs to end, and we shouldn't prolong it.

S: *Is there anything else important or interesting about this scene?*

J: The bridges. I'm standing in the middle of the bridge and it is terrifying. The fall is so far, and there is nothing but black water beneath.

S: *Do you get a sense of what you're doing there?*

J: I came there to throw myself off the bridge.

S: *Why?*

J: I had had enough and had decided I did not want to finish that life.

S: Look down at your feet and tell me what you see.

J: I have the narrow white feet of a women. My toenails are painted a pinkish color; they're chipped. I'm very thin and slender. I feel very upset.

S: Do you get a sense of why you're so upset?

J: I believe there are many different things that have added up, one of them being the loss of someone very close to me.

S: You lost someone close to you?

J: Yes, I feel that I did, and I feel a feeling of abandonment that went along with it. Isolation. Mental illness was what I was told the problem was, but I'd never agreed.

S: You didn't agree?

J: Oh my God, I tried to open up to my true self and begin this process of self-discovery, but everything moved very quickly, and I was committed. People thought I was crazy for saying the things I was saying!

S: What type of things were you saying that people thought were crazy?

J: Oh, the things involving the fact that we're born over and over again, and that we constantly relive. I explained what I knew and what I carried with me, what I dreamed of; and they classified me as crazy.

S: How did that make you feel?

J: Like there was nothing left that I could trust in this world. The isolation of it all led to this.

S: So how did you end up on this bridge?

J: I ran one day. I was able to leave.

S: Did you have to escape?

J: No, I didn't need to escape. I was able to just leave either unnoticed or they no longer had time for me and assumed I was no longer a threat to myself or others. But they did horrible things to me.

S: What did they do to you?

J: They electrocuted me over and over again, and my brain right up here (pointing to where the tumor was) hurts so much right now. I think they lobotomized me. I think they took a piece of my brain out.

S: You don't have to feel any physical discomfort as you talk to me. You can just see this as an observer.

J: They did this so I wouldn't think these things.

S: Did it stop you from thinking those things?

J: No, it just always gave me headaches, and I don't think I was ever the same. I had built a connection to myself, and I'd lost that. I had found the information, and I'd started on my own figuring out what this world really is. And I got really far, and they took it from me. They shocked it out of me and cut it out of me.

S: What happened next?

J: I knew I could never go back, and there was no way to go forward. I threw myself off the bridge, but I didn't make it to the bottom.

S: What happens?

J: They pull me out before I hit.

S: Who pulls you out?

J: The life force? Them? They remove me before I hit the water, but the feeling of falling stays with me always. The drop. The fear of learning what I learned and having them take this away, that was the worst.

S: Let's leave that scene and move back in time in that same lifetime to when you were a child. Be there now. What do you become aware of?

J: It is still New York City. It seems as if it's in the early 60's, maybe late 50's. There are babies in prams all around, and I'm being taken for a walk by my mother in my pram, my stroller, and she's showing me off. She has done my hair up in blond little curls and has dressed me very adorably. But she is using me to get attention for herself.

S: You can feel this? How does this make you feel?

J: Insignificant, even as a very little child I can feel it, and I can see it. I feel about 8 months old. I think she is a single mother and I do not have a father around yet. I think that is what she's doing. I think she is showing me off and searching for someone new to take care of us.

S: Does she meet anyone?

J: She does, and the man she does bring home is not a very good man.

S: Tell me more.

J: Jimmy is his name. He meets us when I am three or four. He's nice at first and then he begins to show his true colors; but by then it's too late and she is married to him. He beats her constantly.

S: Do you see this?

J: I don't try to get involved, but yes. I've learned to hide until it's over. I hide in the closet and stay very still.

S: Does he ever do anything to you?

J: As I get older, he does. Not while I'm younger.

S: What does he do?

J: I start to speak out on days when it looks like he's going to kill her. I try to explain to him that it's not worth it, that he'll go to jail.

S: What happens when you speak out and say this to him?

J: He just starts slapping me, reminds me that I did better when I minded my own business.

S: What happens next?

J: I leave as soon as I'm able to, and I go to live with family friends. It is another mother who has many children but has allowed me to stay there as long as I want to. I only have to check in at my other home every now and then. This other woman gives me the strength to get through it and shows me that not everyone has to end up and act that way. She saw what I was going through, and she related, and in a way, she tries to save me.

S: Is there anything in particular that's important to know about her?

J: She's very forward thinking, and she introduces me to her friend who has made her this way. This friend takes to me very well. I think her name is Julie. And Julie is the one that makes me understand the process of self-discovery. She helps me discover all of who I am, and that I am so much more than the circumstances that are around me.

S: Tell me more about what you discover?

Entering the long-lost continent of Lymuria

My curiosities were piqued as I wondered what she could have uncovered that was so powerful that people would call her crazy. How could learning about self-discovery cause someone to be lobotomized? What I learned next helped me to understand.

J: She helps me to discover some experiences I had before this life.

S: *How do you go about doing that?*

J: She is able to put me into a trance with a candle, and I have to stare at this candle while she says certain things. And all of a sudden, things will appear in my mind and she guides me through them. And I see what has happened and that this isn't my first time on this earth, nor my last.

S: *Is there anything interesting that stands out to you?*

J: Yes, I was a very powerful head of an ancient group of people in the South Pacific. She helped me to remember what happened to me and my child.

S: *What happened to the two of you?*

J: Everyone drowned. I had one daughter. I came from a matriarchal culture where the women are not born of men. There is a process of fertilization that is done via artificial insemination, but the women are never touched directly by the men.

S: *Why is this?*

J: It is the tradition. It is how you continue the line of our people. This was my child; my only child, and she would inherit everything. And then I encountered another race of people who came seeking the powers we held.

S: *What type of powers did you hold?*

J: We held very ancient powers that had been handed off from generation to generation from an early civilization who came to colonize this planet.

S: *What type of people came to colonize this planet?*

J: These were people from a different planet. They had passed down these traditions. We were hundreds of thousands, if not millions strong in numbers. We had everything. It was the most beautiful existence. We had a very fair society. People progressed. It was a constant state of enlightenment of our own beautiful world.

S: *What type of power did you possess?*

J: I was able to manipulate crystals in order to communicate with our ancient ancestors and through that process, keep our people healthy. We never had disease.

S: *How did you do that?*

J: In a cave altar that had been built many eons before there were different sizes of red crystals, and after meditating and placing your hands on them, you could channel their energy. You could see things that have happened, and you could see things that could happen. But they never warned me. They never told me!

S: *Who never warned you?*

J: The crystals, I felt misled. Perhaps it was the manipulation by those who wanted the crystals. I don't know for sure just yet. The people that wanted the crystals killed all my people! They were floating face down in the water! These people who wanted the crystals were able to create a massive explosion in the water, several of them! They destroyed our civilization and took me!

At this point Jen started getting very emotional and I reminded her that she did not have to experience any physical discomfort and could witness this as an observer if she wanted to.

S: *Why did they take you. You said you were the leader?*

J: Yes, and when I tried to explain this memory of a different lifetime to other people, they said I was crazy.

S: *So, after you pulled this memory with the help of Julie, you tried to tell other people about it?*

J: I felt like since I had this memory and had no idea of this memory before, then there was more to the story that perhaps I could learn from other people. But the people I told this to were all phony. They pretended to be interested, but then conspired together to have me committed. I was putting together all the puzzle pieces. I was really breaking through. And they took it from me!

Entering the lost city of Atlantis

At the time, while doing this session I had no idea that this would be a glimpse into Atlantis. It is only upon further inspection that I would learn the name of this place.

S: *What were you working on when they took it from you?*

J: I was wondering why I had been saved and everyone else around me had died.

S: *Did you find out?*

J: I believe I was a prisoner by the people who did this massacre.

S: *You were a prisoner?*

J: For the majority of my life. I can see it now. I can see myself as an old woman with gray hair still in the house they kept me in.

S: *What does this house look like? Can you describe it for me?*

J: It was less like a home and more of an apartment in a high-rise building that had maximum security. There was no way I was getting out of there. It was a little rudimentary on the inside, very basic.

S: *Is there anything interesting that stands out to you there?*

J: Outside the window. I sit by the window and they do have vehicles that can float in the air.

S: *There are vehicles that float in the air? Could you tell me more about them?*

J: They go very fast. I remember being here! It's a very dreary and depressing place.

S: *How do they treat you there?*

J: They took me out on a few occasions. They try ways to extract the information from me.

S: *What information?*

J: They want to be able to manipulate the energy to contact the others. They believed that they were destined to make this contact and receive more knowledge on how to further their technology and their domination. They believed I was the only being left that possessed this information. They felt that if they killed me, then it would be gone. They thought they would just outwait me. They thought I would break.

S: Did you ever break? Did they ever learn?

J: No, and I believe I was there for over sixty years. A prisoner for over sixty years. I wanted to die, but I could not.

S: Why?

J: There was no one else to give this information to, and if I gave it to them, it would be a devastation for the world. I needed to leave it with someone. It couldn't die with me. It was the only reason I couldn't die. I wanted to, I wanted to be with my child. I wanted her back.

S: What happened to your child?

J: There was a tidal wave caused by an atomic type device that the people who captured me set off in strategic places, in rifts underneath the ocean. They had devices that operated like submarines that they placed in these riffs. They had acted as if they were our friends, and then the wave came.

S: Tell me more about this wave.

J: At first I was with many others on the beach looking, looking for where the water had gone. We couldn't understand where the water was pulling out from. Fish everywhere were flopping. Everyone was just standing around looking, wondering. and then I saw it out of the corner of my eye. I saw the wave, and it was massive, it was the size of... you've never seen anything so big in your entire life. There was a rock cliff in front of me and I began to climb as fast as I could climb as everyone just stood there frozen.

S: Where is your daughter?

J: She's not on the beach, she's back at the palace.

S: What happens next?

J: I make it to the top. I'm still running and running. They want to keep me alive. They want me to see their power and how they could destroy everything as they told me they would if I didn't do what they wanted. But I wouldn't believe them. I believed our numbers were greater, and that we would win. I had no idea! My child was swept into something, and the back of her head was impaled onto something sharp, and that is how I found her. Face down in the water with something lodged into the base of her skull. That was the first place I ran. I knew where she was. I don't know why I was able to outrun it and nobody else. I feel like they put me into a bubble or something that made me witness it, but not even get my feet wet.

S: What happened next?

J: They took me. I could see as they took me away, hundreds of thousands of bodies and debris all in the water. There was nothing recognizable left, and in just a minute it was all gone. Everything was destroyed.

S: What kinds of thoughts are going through your mind?

J: Grief, overwhelming, screaming grief!

S: Where do they take you?

J: They take me back to their island. They have an island that's very sophisticated and very advanced.

S: What do they look like?

J: They are very tall people; they're very pale. I think they are very ugly. They're very shrewd. Many of them have very light blondish hair. There is a very negative, competitive nature on this island. People are not very friendly. They are not very helpful towards each other. They are just not very happy people.

S: *They aren't very happy?*

J: No, it's a horrible place, and a horrible place for me. I was very open and free and lived amidst beautiful nature, and this is the complete opposite. It's grey and slate, metal and concrete and you can't even really see the sun.

S: *Why can't you see the sun?*

J: You can some days just not every day.

S: *Why is that?*

J: There is a fog that comes through from their technology.

S: *You said they are very advanced. What do you mean by that?*

J: They have cooking apparatuses that allow you to cook things very quickly. There was a type of energy they used to focus on the food that would cook it as well. The medical technology was really astounding.

S: *Tell me more about that?*

J: They could perform full surgeries. They could manipulate organs and regrow them.

S: *How did they do that?*

J: They understand the usage and practicality of stem cell research and other types of medical practice that we are still not utilizing at this point in history.

S: *They were using stem cell research?*

J: That was one of the reasons they were able to get into the cloning of organs to prolong the life of the individual. They wanted to live forever.

S: *Were they spiritual in any way?*

J: No, they would consider themselves scientists. It was a different type of spirituality though. I can't say no completely. It's just not what I would consider spiritual. There was a deep, deep obsession with the unexplainable phenomenon of certain crystals. They cannot remember how to communicate with their ancestors.

S: *Who do you mean? Who are the ancestors?*

J: The people who seeded them here on this planet. The originating planet.

S: *Tell me more about that.*

J: They came from another planet that had already completed it's evolutionary path. And when those people came to colonize, the need and the lack was so great that it drove them to become these cold, calculating people.

S: *But you knew this knowledge?*

J: Yes. At the time I thought it was our ancestors and the dead who had departed that I was communicating with, but I was definitely able to channel into another realm, perhaps even through a worm hole to those we had originated from.

S: *Were you mistaken? You thought you were talking with someone else?*

J: At the time yes. My people thought it was our dead ancestors that we were communicating with, the ones who had come before us and who had ruled our tribes before, but really it was the ones who seeded us, or even the ones before that. There was a direct channel to another realm, another planet and that was truly what we were tapping into, but we were not aware. Talking to the dead is what they used to call it.

S: Who called it that?

J: My grandmother. She would say "let's talk to the dead today."

S: Tell me more about her.

J: She taught me many things while my mother was in power. My mother taught me many things as well. They were very nurturing, beautiful, powerful women.

S: What do you feel was one of the most important lessons they taught you?

J: The way to treat people, and how to relate to them. A good ruler cannot hold themselves above their people and expect them to obey and worship them just because they are standing above. Being a good ruler is something you must earn, and something you must embody. It is something you must create within yourself that makes people relatable to you and allows them to open their hearts to you being their leader. They want to be led, but they want to know this is the right direction to be led.

S: Were you able to do that?

J: I was.

S: So, with all this knowledge, did you die with it or were you able to find someone to pass it onto?

J: I did. I did something very tricky.

S: What did you do?

J: There was a young girl in the later years of my life who was sent to take care of me. She would cook for me. She must have been about fourteen or fifteen years old. This young girl was from a very lower-class family, not very respected. She had no desire to gain the respect of those around her either, and she saw with clear eyes what her society really was. We developed a very deep friendship, I bestowed on her everything I could.

S: How did you do that?

J: There is a transfer of energy that you can do. Within this I gave her my memories and the path to connecting with the crystals back to that realm. I gave her my blood. I remember the blood. I had to give her my blood in something.

S: What did she do with it?

J: She wore it around her neck and left. I made her leave. I sent her away on a mission and told her not to come back for any reason. I told her to go as far as she could. After it had been transferred, I was ready to complete the rest of my mission.

The Destruction of the lost city of Atlantis

S: What was your mission?

J: I was going to blow the entire civilization up.

S: How were you going to do that?

J: I told the leaders that I was ready to die, and I was ready to pass on the information. So, I simply gave them the wrong information, and with this misinformation, their crystals misfired and caused the most beautiful explosion. It blew the entire civilization off the map.

S: Where did this civilization go?

J: It blew into the sea; it shook and burned. They let me watch it from above.

S: *Tell me more about that?*

J: I was dead, but I watched it from above.

S: *How did you feel as you watched this?*

J: Self-righteous. (a little laugh) I felt complete, good.

S: *What do you mean that the crystals misfired?*

J: Some of the technology they had sought from me was bomb-making technology in order to control other civilizations that they knew of from their explorations, and to control their resources. To threaten one with these bombs would mean an immediate surrender. I simply gave them the calculations for something that would not misfire on someone else but would explode before they had a chance to use it.

S: *Tell me more about this?*

J: I died as the initial explosion blew up.

S: *What happened to the girl and the information that she has?*

J: It does begin there. She took the information north, very far north. I told her to go until she saw snow, and when she saw snow, she would be safe.

S: *Where did she go?*

J: To where you would call northern Europe now, and it (the power) stayed there. It circulated among many people.

S: *What happened next with this girl?*

J: She passed the information down to her children. The legends of Norse Gods stem from this.

S: *Did it infiltrate into society or did it get lost?*

J: It eventually got lost, and I'm one of the last ones left that still has the memory.

S: *So, when Julie was helping you to pull this memory with the candle, how did this make you feel?*

J: It helped with the loneliness and isolation that I'd felt in that life too. Once this memory was found, it felt better. It felt lighter, safer, but it also helped me understand why I felt like I was hiding my whole life up until then. Before this, I'd felt like I was always in hiding, running away from the same experience.

S: *When you reconnected with these memories were you also able to reconnect with those abilities?*

J: Things started getting a little weird at that point.

S: *Tell me more.*

J: I started seeing things clearly for what they really were. The facades around me, the society I was living in felt like it was breaking away every day. I felt that I needed to communicate this with other people, that they were just in their own way, enslaved to this concept of everyday life around us. And if there was something more there for me that was causing this pain, there was something there for others as well, and they also needed to encounter what it was.

S: *So, what happened when you went about sharing this knowledge before you were committed?*

J: I tried to explain it to many people. Most people do not want their world disrupted.

S: Did you convince anyone?
J: I never saw that. I just felt the sting of being labeled crazy which makes you just want to hide again.
S: So, people told you were crazy, what happened next?
J: I think there was a couple of years where I really did try to uncover and go further into it, maybe a year or two. But I don't think I was very old when I threw myself off the bridge. I don't even think I was in my 30's yet.
S: What happened after you passed and threw yourself off the bridge?
J: There are big repercussions when you decide to end your preconceived existence.
S: Tell me more about that. What happens?
J: Suicide is a demerit.
S: Who is holding the points?
J: There is a massive system, a universal system of... what it looks like is taking a rock and putting it in a tumbler...and you're creating this tumultuous experience for the rock, but when it comes out it is a beautiful, polished stone of much more use and much more advancement. And when you stop the process, it causes things to go a little haywire.
S: What were you supposed to do instead of taking your life?
J: I needed to spread this information to people and I took the easy way out.
S: Did you find this out right after you left the body?
J: Yes, you find it out almost before you leave the body, you feel it. You feel the regret right before they snatch you out of it. You recognize it just at that last split second, and then they pull you out of that body.
S: So, as you leave that body, tell me everything you become aware of?
J: It feels like someone with a big hand grabbed me, but instead of grabbing all of me, they grabbed part of me. So part of you still falls, and you know this, and something pulls part of you upwards and you kind of just float there. And it's almost as if it's a download immediately. You start processing what's just happened, and everything that's just led up to it, and you start to realize that you may have just made yourself have to do this all over again.
S: Did you decide after this to do this again?
J: It was always going to happen. If you failed to complete something that you have wanted to complete, you will continue to redo it until you have completed it.
S: So, did you decide on a life when you would complete this?
J: This is the next one!

At this point using Dolores Cannon's method of QHHT I called in the subconscious to ask questions about the client, and about why they showed her the lifetime that she just witnessed.

S: Why did you show her that lifetime as the women who took her own life? What were you trying to tell her?
J: That that is not the path to take this time around.
S: What do you mean?

J: Suicide and self-isolation.

S: *Does she understand this now?*

J: Yes.

S: *What information do you want her to take from this lifetime?*

J: It is important for her to encounter who she is and to uncover what she has been hiding for hundreds of thousands of years. And to share it, and to allow the evolution of the earth to continue with this information. This is why we brought her to you. She needs to understand that there is a larger contract created through many of her lives that still must be fulfilled.

S: *What is the contract?*

J: She must embrace this new way of being. The only way to go full circle to what we once were and to understand who we truly are is to dive into this it, and to not fear the ostracization that comes with it.

S: *So, she has to really dive into this. What exactly do you mean by this? Do you mean the knowledge that she holds within herself?*

J: Yes.

S: *What do you want her to do with it?*

J: She must find a way to explain this to people in a way that is comfortable to her, that brings her strength instead of repercussion and the labeling of crazy. She must find it within herself, and like a good leader, make this relatable to those who would like to follow in this direction.

S: *How can she best go about doing that?*

J: Through her writing.

S: *She said that she wants to write a book. Should she write a book about this?*

J: She should write many books about this, many. There are so many beings helping her with this. There are so many that it may be overwhelming at times.

S: *Tell me more?*

J: Also, there are many experiences of other lifetimes that are all combined to help bring this information further.

S: *How should she start the writing? Is there a way you want her to start this process?*

J: There needs to be an opening of a channel that is blocked. She's only able to get dribs and drabs of information from it. But if the channel is opened and cleared out the information will come very steadily and readily.

S: *Why has this channel been blocked?*

J: It has been blocked for many reasons. She felt that this opening was what caused her destruction and has put a very tight block on it so that she wouldn't be condemned in this life.

S: *Does she need this block anymore?*

J: No, and she now knows this.

S: *Since she doesn't need this anymore, could you unblock this channel for her now?*

J: Yes, we're unblocking it now.

S: *What will she notice after this?*

J: She will notice that information will flow freely from our side to her side. It will allow her to understand the bigger picture of how the story must be placed.

S: *Could you start a body scan on her?*

J: There is still a lot of tension in the brain.

S: *What is causing that?*

J: The tumor. However, it's no longer needed anymore.

S: *What was the purpose of the tumor?*

J: To get her here, to see you, and to go within, to uncover these memories and fulfill her purpose.

S: *Has she learned everything she needs to learn from having this tumor?*

J: She has. We can release it now.

S: *How are you doing that? I'm always curious.*

J: We are draining it. It will start shrinking now.

S: *What will she notice?*

J: She will feel better right away, and the next time she meets with the medical team that she works with they will be astounded that it will have shrunken completely. They will have no explanation for this.

S: *Is there anything else you would like to tell Jen at this time?*

J: The time is now.

In the months that followed Jen's session, not only had her brain swelling subsided, but vitality came back to her body and mind. She was even able to get pregnant and give birth to a healthy baby girl, another feat that was deemed impossible by her medical team. It was during this time that I learned that I had passed my exam and was now a level 3 practitioner, meaning a mastery of this field. This was fantastic life-changing news for me as this meant that not only would I be booked with more QHHT clients, but I would also be invited to assist with the many classes the QHHT organization hosts all over the world.

My life had just made an exciting turn. As predicted, I soon was busy seeing clients on a daily basis. From this new surge of clients an interesting phenomenon seemed to be occurring. People who had no connection, and who had never met one another were saying similar things about two ancient civilizations in their hypnosis sessions. From what I was starting to understand through my clients' sessions, Lemuria (also known as Lymuria), or Amun as it was called then, was located in the South Pacific, and encompassed the land that is now Easter Island and stretched toward South America. Many maintain that it was a large island where the right to rule was passed down through the bloodline of a female monarchy. Always described as a very comfortable happy place, the people of Lymuria valued compassion and spirituality. It would come to seem that while their world was ripped apart 25,000 years ago, many souls have come back again in our current world and still hold the trauma from the wave that destroyed Amun.

CHAPTER 2: UFO CRASHES AND THE BEGINNING OF CIVILIZATION ON EARTH

At this point Jen and I felt compelled to work together more. If spreading this information was her purpose in this life, then we needed to find out more about what this information was and why this was so important. I understood that information was given to us, not all at once, but through patience and diligence; and so I understood that Jen and I would work together multiple times to retrieve this knowledge. We decided that we needed to start from the beginning with her memories of that lifetime. We wanted to recount the whole life in chronological order to make sure we didn't miss anything that was important, or that needed to be shared with the world. Thinking that Jen would be regressed back to the beginning of the life in Lymuria, we were both surprised when she instead went to a different life, in a different body as the commander of an extra-terrestrial ship coming to Earth for the first time. This was what we uncovered.

S: Let's drift and float to the beginning, the start of the story that you need to uncover. What do you become aware of?
J: It's cold, very, very cold. There's a lot of coldness stored in what feels like a rock in front of me. A very dark, cold segmented rock.
S: Describe it to me.
J: The rock is cold and segmented with vertical lines.
S: Look down at your body and see if you have feet there.
J: Yes, I have a type of silver boot on my feet.
S: How do these boots feel on your feet?
J: They have water inside of them. They're wet, and they are uncomfortable, and it's very cold.
S: Tell me more.
J: The water adds an extra chill.
S: What are you wearing on the rest of your body?
J: I'm wearing a blue, close-to-the-skin lycra material, almost stretchy fabric. It fits to the body. It's almost a seamless one piece. And the blue is a very specific color blue that almost seems to have a shimmer of silver in it as well.
S: What about the top part of your body?
J: The same one-piece jumpsuit covers my body up to the neck. It covers half of the neck and all the way down to the cuffs of my arms. It's all the same color, but there is a small design by the breast area that looks like a crescent moon with three circles next to it. And that design is a slightly darker silver grey.
S: What does your face look like?
J: It looks like it's pale white, very pale actually. There's no facial hair. I'm very clean shaven. I have blond hair, with an undertone of red in it, like a strawberry blond that mixes in with white blond. Very light eyebrows, blue, green eyes.
S: Tell me about your eyes?
J: They're almond shaped and pin up at the edges, but not too big. Slightly larger than the eyes I have currently.

S: *Do the symbols on your jumpsuit mean anything to you?*

J: It is the symbol for the space exploration program, the program that I'm involved in. It's for exploration.

S: *How do you feel about that?*

J: I feel very proud of it; I feel that it's an elite program. I look at it and I feel just a surge of pride within me. The exploration of continuing our kind is the first goal.

S: *What happened to your kind? Can they not continue where you're from?*

J: There is a serious depletion of resources, and we have been around for a very long time. We have accumulated not an enemy, but a source of competition over our resources, and we fear they will become an enemy as the resources dwindle. We've had an advanced society for a very long time and the thing that we have become most reliant on is a type of mineral/crystal. We've just exhausted our resources of this mineral/ crystal. And there's truly no way to create this in a laboratory. This mineral/crystal has to be found.

S: *It has to be found?*

J: It has to be found or it can be delivered to a planet on an asteroid. It can be formed either when an asteroid crashes into a planet or during the early days of the formation of a planet when many particles crash into it. So, we have gone to other planets where we have found it and have mined those efficiently over the millennia. But we have found this new place, this place you call Earth, and it is rich with this resource.

S: *What do you do with this resource? Why do you want it so badly?*

J: What it allows us to do is to create another dimension, another realm. It allows us to create or transfer into it, and we have existed within both. It seems it is a religious, or a right of passage. In order to become enlightened, you must make this journey. If you don't make the journey, then you do not function within our society because you are not enlightened to it.

S: *So it's used mostly for enlightenment? Correct?*

J: Yes, and this was the ultimate goal.

S: *If you lose this material, then what would happen to your people?*

J: They would de-evolve and the new ones (it is not children, that's not the word)...the new people would not become enlightened and we would lose this very valuable asset that has taken us a very long time to understand and to experience. It is what keeps us at peace with one another.

S: *Can you tell me more about this asset?*

J: I see it as a dull red gemstone that is found within a silvery type of substance. The silvery substance is important for the transfer of energy. The gemstone and the silvery substance need to work together to create this. I would describe it like a laser, or better yet Tesla's stream of energy that you would see, or you could also describe it as a lightning bolt. It has to be done in some type of circular stone area where it will hit the gem and refract off, and as it does, it shoots off these larger stone slabs and creates a vortex. It creates a very specific type of swirling opening. You can go in, and you can come out, and you will never be the same when you come out.

S: *What happens when you go in? Could you describe it for me?*

J: There is a very heavy dark inkiness that you feel as you cross through. And then you start to feel as if the parts of your body are drifting away from the core of your body. You feel your arms and your legs leave, and you feel as if you're just floating there. As you finally relax, as you float, you feel as if you are no longer part of your body and your body pulls away from you. You are then shown the purpose of the Universe.

S: What is the purpose of the Universe?

J: There is a lot, and I can remember parts. There is **a huge connectivity and a continuum, a figure eight that allows for things to consistently happen, but in different ways.** There is a very deep bright light that shines throughout you. There is a level of orchestration, a game. There is…it's very vague. They're taking this memory as fast as I'm pulling it, and I'm trying to pull this memory as fast as they are taking it.

S: Is there a reason they don't want you to remember this?

J: We're not capable of understanding it yet, and I'm having trouble understanding it myself.

S: Can you tell me more about this enlightenment process?

J: The first step is to understand that life is like a game, and to understand how old this game is and that it has been going on for longer than human beings can fully comprehend in the aspect of time. We have consistently created new realms and planets, and have consecutively inhabited them. And in each furtherment there is something new to be learned. It is not the same lesson to be learned. It is something new to be uncovered that furthers us.

S: How did this get started?

J: There was a group in the very beginning; it was not one. There were a few of them. And they felt empty inside. They felt nothing and they wanted to feel something. And they began something that involved creating in their own image. They are a group that is eternal; a group that does not have gender. They are a governing group. And this is a grand never-ending experiment.

S: What was the experiment meant to do?

J: The experiment was done out of loss, out of need, out of the desire for company, for things to be done around them. I feel they suffered a great loss. I feel like they were survivors, and they had the infinite ability to start again and to continue. And this is what has come from it. But there was a deep melancholy to the group. The experiment was not being done out of joy and happiness, or even malicious intent.

S: Tell me more?

J: There was a sadness that led them to starting this domino effect of enlightened humans or creatures.

S: What exactly were they hoping to get out of that?

J: A recreation of what they once had. Though we are still nowhere near what they had before.

S: What did they have before?

J: They didn't really have bodies, but more of a gaseous cloud of color. They expressed themselves like a cloud that has different colors to it. And they could sense the colors, and they could communicate this way.

S: What colors?

J: I see purple and blues, muted pastel colors. Some have grey to them, and a little bit of yellow. But they wanted to do this experiment. And through this experiment this never-ending, unyielding figure eight of creation was created.

S: *When you get into this vortex, are you able to see all of this?*

J: In different levels. They give you a little bit at first and then have you leave. You are sent to process that, and then you are allowed to go back and receive more, if you feel that you would like to receive more. Not everyone chooses to receive more. But everyone has to go at least once.

S: *Everyone has to go at least once?*

J: It makes your cerebellum balance to a non-violent, non-hostile, non-confrontational state. It removes all insecurity from people, the root cause of the majority of our wars and conflicts.

S: *So, insecurity causes these things?*

J: Yes, and this is a defense mechanism for the people on this planet, to keep our society from breaking out into all out chaos. As long as we are shown this information there is no need to battle with others or yourself.

S: *Why is that? Because your insecurities are removed?*

J: You feel how connected you are in every aspect, because you realize that it was all created from one giant ball of light that breaks itself down into creating everything. And the connectivity... you can feel the connectivity pulse through your body like you're being electrocuted. It will not kill you but will just shock sense into you.

S: *So, it's like a shock, and you feel how connected you really are?*

J: Yes, to everyone around you and you no longer feel the need to harm or to judge, or to compare.

S: *Are you essentially everyone you see? Is everything connected in that way?*

J: Yes, and then there is a great love that opens up. It opens up for yourself first and then for those you see around you. After the first time you go through the vortex, you can look at someone and see their struggles and what they go through. The compassion that comes from it negates the fear you would've once had about these people and it bands you together.

S: *How many times have you gone into this Vortex?*

J: Seven times, and that is why I was chosen to go on the expedition to find more.

S: *Now that you're on this expedition, what did you find?*

J: Nothing. It would've seemed a failure at first glance, but I was meant to find nothing.

S: *Why is that?*

J: From this perspective I can see how it plays out and that I was not meant to find more of this specific gem and mineral.

S: *Why?*

J: I was meant to begin a new colony.

S: *Where was this colony?*

J: Earth.

S: *How did you find this planet?*

J: This planet had been found and it had been monitored for quite a while as we watched the development from amoeba to man take place with certain assistance.

S: *Tell me more about this assistance? What was the process?*

J: Once the conditions were found on this planet that we understood would evolve into better conditions, the seeds were planted. Single-celled organisms were sprinkled into the different parts of the ocean. The ocean was vast at this time. There was very little land and a majority of this land was uninhabitable. There was also very little oxygen in the ozone layer within it.

S: *Was oxygen created or brought in?*

J: Over time there was a natural growth and progression. There was a continuous growth under the ocean for years, and years, and years because there is always evolution. But evolution always needs a push, a helping hand.

S: *How is that done?*

J: Through genetic modifications that are made and implanted into certain organisms that allow for a different reaction to happen in the organism's next procreation.

S: *Who does this?*

J: There are many different scientists who have perfected this already. Many of the experiments were carried out on our home planet and then transferred over to this one.

S: *How were they taken back and forth?*

J: In a very simple saline solution that was used for the transfer of many of these organisms. It is the same solution that we're still using to create within. The most important thing to understand from this experiment is that evolution on it's own is a very powerful force, but it can take quite a while. All that was done was that we sped it up in some circumstances.

S: *Which circumstances did you speed up?*

J: After the Earth had cooled, and the land formations began there were very large trees everywhere. Larger than anything you could truly imagine. When these started to sprout up we went in and changed certain things within the small amoebas, the little organisms, these tadpoles if you will. And then the next generation suddenly had the ability to breathe outside of the water for a little while.

S: *How do you manipulate the genes?*

J: Through gene splicing, gene manipulation. Nothing that they didn't already have, just a little more advanced than what they had. It wasn't for all of them. It was spread out and it was varied and if you just give it enough time, it takes it's own natural course. With a helping hand, it speeds it up a little bit.

S: *How do your scientists know how to do this?*

J: It has been passed down through the subconscious collective memory and un-earthed as we configured and conferred with the other dimension.

S: *Were there a lot of beings working on this project?*

J: There was an entire agency, hundreds, thousands, perhaps.

S: *Can you describe what these creator beings look like?*

J: Very similar to how I looked, tall, very pale skin, very lithe in appearance, and very light features. They almost look like giant Nordic individuals.

S: *Where is your home planet? How far away is it from Earth?*

J: If you were to go by miles, it would not be achievable. You wouldn't be able to go so far, but if you were to use a dimension hopper, black hole, a Segway to that planet. It would not take long at all. It's a very quick journey using the right path.

S: *Is that how you go back and forth?*

J: Transport is the easiest part of the experiment. This experiment would not have worked if we did not have the right conditions to begin with. It is very difficult to create the conditions and then manipulate the genes. The conditions must exist first for the gene manipulation to be effective.

S: *How were the conditions created?*

J: The conditions were not created through us. They were a result of the way this planet was created. Some planets are habitable for some things and some are habitable for others. There is a great variance in this. You may look at a planet and think it is completely useless and void of life and resources, but it is only that way for a human. For another it could be a very specific place to continue their civilization. So, for our people we needed water, salt, and we needed oxygen to eventually inhabit this planet.

S: *So, the goal was to eventually inhabit this planet?*

J: It is always a policy to have a backup planet in the event of the unthinkable.

S: *What is the unthinkable?*

J: That there is no longer the ability to sustain our people and our life. It is not unfathomable. It is something we're doing right now as a people. And continuing.

S: *So, Earth is your backup?*

J: Our laboratory and backup, I didn't understand at the time what I was being sent for, but it was to begin the colonization under the guise of exploration.

S: *How did you begin this colonization?*

J: There was a deliberate malfunction of the ship and we crashed sideways into a very hard type of rock. We crashed into a place that has very dark cold water and our ship rolled into the water and it remains there to this day. We had never been prepared for the crash, the cold, or for the trauma. Some of us did not make it at all.

S: *What happened to them?*

J: The impact broke their necks, snapped them, and they dangled there. It was terrifying, and I had to stay calm. I had to lead them out of there. We were not prepared. I was not prepared. We had to open the door as the water rushed in and pushed us back up against the back of the ship. I remember feeling the metal, the buttons, the things on the wall that drove the ship. I remember feeling the metal against me as the water pushed me into it. It was freezing.

S: *You could feel the cold?*

J: The cold was unmeasurable. It was frozen. But we were able to get out.

S: *How did you get out?*

J: I was able to open my eyes under the water, and after the initial shock, I was able to grab a few hands and we banded together as we had been taught in our extraction regiment.

S: *You had practiced an extraction regiment?*

J: Almost like army training, getting out of our ship in case of an accident was something we had practiced. Our training kicked in and allowed for a few of us to swim out. There were six of us that got out, two who died on impact, and I think one of us died after we got out, from hypothermia.

S: So, what happened next?

J: We sat in shock, freezing, and shivering, not knowing what to do.

S: Had you been told any of this in your training?

J: We were prepared for certain things, but we were not prepared for the cold or the water, and we had nothing with us that would allow us to use our technology. We did not know how to survive. We did not know how to make fire, and we stayed this way for two days. After the shock initially wore off, we started to just wander together. We walked to not die, to stay warm, to keep our bodies moving, and our blood flowing. We walked and we walked. And there was great distress amongst everyone. We didn't believe we would find anything. We didn't know what we were looking for.

S: You didn't know what you were looking for?

J: We didn't think there was anything to look for. And my crew started to turn on me.

S: How did they turn on you? What did they do?

J: They wanted to die, and I wouldn't let them. They didn't believe that there was anything worth continuing this journey for… and then we met a human being.

S: You met a human?

J: She came out of nowhere.

S: What did she look like?

J: Very hairy, very primitive, with a very light, light brown skin color. She had dark curly hair, a huge mess of it, and she was in shock when she saw us.

S: She was?

J: She had never seen anything that looked or even resembled anything like us.

S: What did she do when she saw you?

J: She slowly started to back up; she had been gathering wood. I fell on my knees and I begged her. I begged her for help. She seemed to understand from the gesture that we were not going to hurt her, and we needed help. And she held her hand out, with her palm out open and stretched out, as if to say wait here. And not much long after she came back with several people, a clan, a group of others. Very primitive, very basic, like the first humans.

S: Tell me more about them?

J: You could still see a little ape in them. You could see a little primate in their features. The eyes, the cheeks, the ears, all still had that shape. The humped posture as well, the hairiness, they were very, very hairy.

S: Was the hair all over the body?

J: For the women it was not as much on the face or chest, but on the legs and arms heavily. And the head tremendously. They had very big eyebrows that were all joined together, almost to the point where you really couldn't see the forehead on many of them.

S: What happened next?

J: They brought us to a fire. We were so hungry.

S: Did they feed you? If so, what was it like?

J: It was a mash of roots that had been boiled with some water, kind of like a potato soup that you just ate with your hands.

S: *What did it taste like to you?*

J: It was bland, but it was the feeling of filling that emptiness that we needed. And we all got sick from it. Not because it was bad, just because we were all so hungry at that point that we couldn't hold it down. And we had to show them we were apologetic towards wasting this food. They were upset at first, thinking that we did not like it, but we were just traumatized and starved.

S: *What happened next?*

J: At first they were a little suspicious of us, not understanding. But after a while, they allowed us to build our own little camp near theirs, but not with theirs. And then I began to spend time with the young women who found us.

S: *You did?*

J: We could not understand each other but we could communicate through sign language and body language. But there was a lot we could not say.

S: *Why did you spent a lot of time with her?*

J: There was a lot to learn and it was very lonely.

S: *How did you feel with her?*

J: It was a break from the constant struggle of figuring out what's next. It was a very peaceful little break. And it helped me to focus because it would allow me a distraction from this larger problem. And I could focus on something very simple and very basic in communicating with her.

S: *Tell me more about that? What did you feel was the largest problem?*

J: What do we do? How do we get back home? How do we even get back to the ship? Are we stuck here, or is this just a challenge for us to get back?

S: *What did you decide to do?*

J: When the weather warmed, I tried to swim back under the water to the ship, but I was not successful. I could not hold my breath long enough to get in there, to get anything useful. It was then that we realized that there was no hope. There was no one coming back for us. There was no way to communicate with our home planet. No way for them to even see a crash site because it was under water. We were just stuck, and we began to talk amongst ourselves about how we would even continue. And we realized we were just going to have to assimilate and breed with them, and this was our new life.

S: *How did that make you feel?*

J: Horrible, like I had let them all down, let my team members down. They said I had given up, and they were not interested in breeding with monkeys, and I explained to them so many times that this was the only way that we would continue our journey through assimilation and procreation. They did not agree.

S: *What happened after that?*

J: I began to explain and show them that it could be done, and we could be happy. And so, with the young women we befriended in the beginning, the one who found us, I began to instigate a relationship with her. But, it was not what these primitive people were used to.

S: *It wasn't?*

J: No, their way was more rough. You took what you wanted, rather than asked. And my approach was not seen as a characteristic of something they wanted there.

S: They didn't like how you approached her?

J: No, they would prefer as a man that I would be very dominant, and I was not. We had understood in our upbringing, from where we were from, that relationships were more of an equality and a balance, but for them it was more of a take it if you want it. And it caused problems because they did not see this as equal and it was more of a step down for them rather than a step towards mating. But I was very persistent and eventually we began a very strong relationship. But the problem was that there was always an element of miscommunication. We still could not speak a language together. And she never felt like she was given what she thought she would be getting within her culture.

S: What was that? What did she expect and want?

J: That dominance, that overbearing, club you and drag you into a cave mentality from a mate.

S: She wanted this?

J: It was what she expected, and it really was what they revered as true manhood. This caused many problems for us and there were also many children born that did not make it. They would come out, and they would not live. They would live for a few moments, and then they would die. It took its toll on her.

S: What did these children look like?

J: They were hybrids. They were, in my eyes beautiful, but in her culture's eyes, they were deformed and unacceptable.

S: How did that make you feel?

J: Horrible, because this is what I promised as our only chance to my people, and it still wasn't working out. Finally, she left with another man from another tribe. She was heavily pregnant with my child, and she didn't expect for that one to live either, but I know now that it did. It was the only one that lived. I didn't see that during my life, only as an after perspective.

S: You didn't know it then?

J: No, one by one we all grew old and died.

S: What about the rest of your crew? Did they end up creating hybrids as well?

J: No, I was the only one. They wouldn't do it; they thought it was beneath them. They thought that there was no point, especially when they saw all of my children die, one after another. There were four of them; the fifth one was the one that made it.

S: What was the one who made it like?

J: She was a girl. She carried heavy characteristics of my side and it seems as if she was ostracized heavily by her community because of it. They saw her as very different, an alien.

S: That was how they saw her?

J: Yes, but she had many children.

S: She did? Tell me more about that.

J: Yes, and her children had many, and those children had many. And it all went back to that one child. But I never saw her; I never saw my child or her mother again. I just watched those others that had arrived with me die, one after another. They just gave up hope; that is what killed them. Their heart gave out with their will to live. Only one survived.

S: *How did they die?*

J: It would happen quickly. The first one died of just malaise; his heart gave out. One of them jumped off a very high cliff, and the others created an illness within themselves that allowed them to excuse themselves from this life.

S: *They created the illness? How did they do that?*

J: Through the general feeling of depression and hopelessness, they were able to attract illness to themselves very quickly. And within that they were gone.

S: *What happened to you?*

J: I didn't give up hope until after she left.

S: *What happened after she left?*

J: I went crazy. I remember running around on these paths that the humans would make. There were huge ferns, ferns the size of me that were all around on either side of the path. I was just running around thinking I could find her somewhere and I could bring her back. I kept thinking that I could do this; I could be a brute, whatever she needs. If I need to just knock her to the ground to make her feel accepted by society, I will do it. I will do it. I have nothing else; I have to find her. And it was not a deep love. It was not a love of my life situation, it was just the only thing I had left.

S: *What happened to you?*

J: I ended up dying alone in a cave, curled up.

S: *OK, just drift and float away from that lifetime now and look at it from a different perspective. Why did you crash your ship?*

J: That was the mission. It was to begin interacting with those singled celled amoebas that had evolved to that point. We had to create it in a way where it was a hybridization between what would naturally grow and prosper and what we were bringing to the planet. The conditions were slightly different on our planet, and we needed to create a race of people that would be able to thrive on this planet. That was the mission. Though, I was the last one to realize it.

S: *How do you feel now looking back at this life?*

J: I feel that I accomplished my mission. It was a very difficult life, full of loneliness, and I felt as if I was a failure. But it was anything but. Looking back it was the beginning of everything. That was the beginning of this planet being groomed- that first baby that survived. She was the key to the success. Because if she could live, then this was not a waste. This experiment was all validated!

S: *What happened to the human race after she had multiple babies?*

J: The intelligence levels rose and with the intelligence comes the advances in technology, advances in language, advances in expression. And you must have a full combination in all of these things in order for a society to become enlightened and in order to transfer into the next phase as a society. It is not something that could be done by simple-minded beings.

S: *How many times were there crashes like yours?*

J: There were many. When I was sent out, there were possibly fifty other ships that were sent out with crews as well. We were all supposed to crash in different spots all around the globe in order to see where the best place for these conditions to thrive would be. That is why now you see people looking so different, yet sharing similar traits. The elements would affect the hybrids differently throughout the years and that would alter the way they looked. For example, those who crash landed in colder places would develop different features over the years than those who crash landed in warmer climates. When the hybridization would happen, it would cause these unique features to surface. Early man looked more like half human, half primate. Yet as the hybridization continued, more and more hybrids began to show different traits such as elongated foreheads, a different shape of the skull to accommodate a different shaped brain and different eye colors. Light colored eyes are a direct result of the hybridization process. We were the first planet though that started doing this, then other planets followed and decided to do it as well.

S: *Is it possible to look at someone's face and tell where they originate?*

J: While that is possible to an extent, humans are a mix of all the races now. Only the dominate gene will still be noticeable.

I had heard from another client under hypnosis that light eyes were a result of the hybridization project- a confirmation of this session with Jen. I wanted to know more about this and so we continued with more questions.

S: *Tell me more about this experiment?*

J: What took us to this planet seems like a very good place to begin this explanation.

S: *What do you mean by that? What is this experiment exactly?*

J: A repetition, a cyclical creation of environment for growth and expansion. This is created over, and over, and over again.

S: *It just keeps going?*

J: This is the most recent beginning.

S: *Was there ever a beginning?*

J: It is an infinite beginning. It is always existing simultaneously and running concurrently with the time and the moment. Everything is happening simultaneously even though it feels as if there is a never-ending gap, almost like a Russian doll with many dolls within itself. And then, within itself, it creates more, we are deep within that Russian doll at this point.

S: *How was the Earth created then?*

J: There was a massive explosion that was provoked, a series of something similar to atoms splitting that happened.

S: *Was this on purpose?*

J: Yes.

S: *Who made this happen?*

J: This was part of the original group that I was talking about before. They are those who dictate when and where we will begin a new dimensional universe.

S: *What else happened to create the Earth?*

J: There was just a very big explosion that catapulted everything into a centrifugal motion and this allowed it to attract like to like, and to create things. It is still the same underlying magnetism that we use in our daily lives. The like-to-like galaxy.

S: *It was the magnetism that attracted everything together?*

J: There is always an element of magnetism in every dimension, in every universe, in every creation. It is what we use to pull like to like. It is why you find dirt in clumps together and not specks littered all around. It is what brings a tree together, what brings a school of fish together. Like to Like.

S: *After the Earth was formed, what happened next?*

J: There was a very long period of formation and cooling, and then it was hot.

S: *It was hot?*

J: When there is that much motion, there is heat that is released from the creation and motion. The friction of that creates heat. And after that, there was a vast cooling; then the beginning of the sprinkling of cells, seeds if you will, were spread out to create. Some grew, some did not. Then, the manipulation began, and we are where we are.

S: *What about the dinosaurs? What was the purpose for them?*

J: They are a terrific source of fuel for the technology you have become dependent on.

S: *Was that their purpose?*

J: It was their main purpose. After they fulfilled their purpose, they were no longer needed and were de-evolved.

S: *How was that accomplished and why?*

J: With the dinosaurs the conditions were not right for our species to prosper. We needed things to eat, but they were not the easiest to catch or to hunt. There were too many jumps in their evolutionary process that we could not explain, that we could not trust. It was found wisest to postpone development slightly and to eradicate this danger.

S: *How did you get rid of them?*

J: There were several tactics that were used. One was a giant explosion that we used in order to alter their eating habits and stress them out. They had a great fear of fire that caused mass panic, and disease. Massive amounts of disease was shipped in that was specific to their breeds.

S: *What type of disease?*

J: What could be called a virus now, but these are not things that would affect humans. We were very careful about what we brought in because we didn't want it to become uncontained. We already realized we had brought things in that we did not want, and so we were very careful about this extermination. There were some dinosaurs we saw as valuable and we liked in many ways the taste of them, so we slowly de-evolved them into different animals that were harmless in many ways.

S: *What animals did you like the taste of?*

J: Chickens were once very vicious dinosaurs. They tasted very good.

S: *How did you make them smaller?*

J: By taking away their resources and their fresh air. It makes them smaller and weaker, less aggressive. And it's something you do slowly over time; it's not something you rush. It's something that has to be done very naturally, this instigation, or they won't survive. We've learned this from the past. Things must be given time.

S: *If you don't give it time, it doesn't work?*

J: Every time, if you push it, it doesn't come out the way you want it to.

S: *In human time, how long would that take?*

J: Probably a good hundred thousand years.

S: So, these animals were created for food. What about the other animals?

J: Some were created for spectatorship, like the large beasts. We realized that when they ate certain foods it would make them taste different. This was not a world where cows and pigs existed. This was not a place where we were looking for a quick, small domestication of herding small animals. We were looking for large animals that we could hunt and that could feed many.

S: What was one of the first?

J: Something that looks almost like a woolly mammoth with large tusks. I see it being like a twenty-story building compared to people who look about five feet tall.

S: So, one of the main purposes of these animals was to be food. How did the primitive people know to eat the animals?

J: They understood as they had evolved themselves that certain things were very edible and certain things were likely to kill them. They understood through trial and error with the foliage and greenery around them. Animals were first introduced to their diet after lightning strikes caused fires in some areas and some of these animals got caught in the fires. And after these fires were gone, the people would explore the areas and they would find these cooked animals, and they began to experiment. If it was not too long after, the smell was pleasing. And they began to realize that they felt differently when they ingested the body of these animals, and they became more powerful because of the additional protein which led to greater brain growth, and stamina. They began to evolve because of that. This is all a very long, long process. It had to be done correctly.

S: After animals were introduced to humans, what was next?

J: The use of certain specific things within nature as medicine.

S: Like what?

J: They began to notice that what they were eating would change the way their body would react to certain things, that different flowers and different roots would make them feel differently. Some could kill you all together. There began a mental record of what did what.

S: A mental record?

J: Because they didn't have writing, or even a concept of what that was, or where to begin. There was an amazing memory for these people. It must've been a very big part of the brain that we have closed down a bit.

S: How was this memory passed down?

J: Through the subconscious and through birth. My child could recall at a certain age many of the things that I already knew, for instance. And you could pass it on. The strongest link was from mother to daughter in the XX chromosome. You could find a direct link to this knowledge from the female lineage and from there the people with the most knowledge became the most important to the group because of their knowledge.

S: Tell me more about that?

J: This particular knowledge was invaluable; it could save other's lives. And while brute force and strength had been the commanding factor of who had been leading groups of people, this began to change as well.

S: So, the people with more memory became the leaders?

J: Yes, and since the women were the ones who could carry and pass on the information, you began to see a matriarchal culture emerging as the first true leaders of that civilization because of this ability to pass the information that could save lives and benefit lives around them. They were natural and fair leaders. And it was not a sheer domination that guided them, but the promise of health that did. And people grew healthier and lived longer and had safer pregnancies and childbirths because of this knowledge, and it became highly respected and coveted.

As Jen was recounting this lifetime, she seemed to be describing the history of the feminine rule and the beginning role they had in our forgotten history and in our society.

S: *Could you give me an example of what type of plants were used for health benefits?*
J: A beautiful white flower that grew among reeds in water. It was collected in the spring, then dried up and ground into a tea. It was something to use in order to bring down pain for people. Pain was a big factor whether it be a tooth ache or childbirth. The controlling of pain was the first thing that we looked for.
S: *What other types of plants did you use?*
J: The barks of trees were found to be filled with things that could be distilled into a tea and were very beneficial for people. Some roots could also be mashed up and cause hallucinogenic effects for people.
S: *Was this beneficial in any way?*
J: It was, and it wasn't at the same time. It was good to know what these things were so that they could be avoided if they were not desired because many misunderstandings would occur from taking them without understanding what they were. And from understanding what they were, many used them for enlightenment purposes and for distractions. What we would eventually call religions was spurred from this.
S: *What happened when they took these hallucinogenics?*
J: They would see things they couldn't understand, and they would place these things as something higher than themselves, something governing them, something above them.
S: *Were these really just hallucinations?*
J: Yes.
S: *What about emotions during that time? Were the emotions of people developed?*
J: At that time there were very few and primitive emotions. There was jealousy, rage, sadness and grief. Happiness was kind of different, it was more of an appreciation and less of a joy for a long time, just a general satisfaction. And from better conditions and better knowledge, we then grew our emotions like joy and happiness. **When conditions exist in one way for a very long time, the emotions will mimic the conditions.**
S: *What was the biggest threat to the people of that time?*
J: The biggest threats were the elements and the animals around them. They were not as likely to become ill with disease.
S: *They weren't?*
J: At first no. It started from those of us that came from other planets, falling ill for many different reasons. And it suddenly became apparent to them that they too could fall sick like this. And from the illnesses of others that they saw they became susceptible as well.

S: What did people start to do then if they had an illness?
J: They would drink these teas and tinctures that the people with the knowledge would find. If they couldn't drink, they would make poultices with leaves and it would be absorbed through the skin.

S: Were these effective?
J: If there was enough belief on both ends, then it would be very effective. But if someone wanted to die, they would die. Wanting to continue is a very big part of the development of the species. There is no medicine to save you if you do not want to live.

Chapter 3: *THE FOUNDER OF ATLANTIS*

One of the questions that had been burning in the back of my mind was how Atlantis found its way into being. All great places must have a beginning, but I was not clear on where or when that was for Atlantis. I had Jen join me for another session to better understand the delicate history that is Atlantis.

S: Let's drift back to that lifetime when you were a commander from a different planet on the ship that just crashed. You said earlier that one of your crew survived? Could you tell me more about this?

J: Yes, I see the large ferns all around us. I see him as well. He's always angry! He needs me constantly. He needs a friend, but he won't admit it. He's always around and always complaining and nagging, whining. It irritates me, but he needs me and he and I both know that. I think I need him as well. We seem stuck and bound to each other as well. I'm very irritated with him.

S: You are?

J: Yes, he's so frustrating to deal with because he knows what we came here to do. He knows what we came to accomplish and now that we're here and we have no choice but to finish this, he wants to leave and he wants to go. He wants to see what else is out there but we have a perfectly fine situation in front of us. He just wants to live by himself. He even built this little house made out of slabs of stone. There is a hole in it that he climbs into, and he stays in there by himself. He has a little fire inside to keep him warm.

S: Tell me more.

J: He goes back to the ship with me, and we dive into the water when the weather warms up. We go back months later after the crash, after we have set up our camp. The ship crashed into the quarry and we decide to go and swim down to it to see if we can get back any of our equipment or see if there are more of the red crystals down there. I remember the water was still very cold, and the second I jumped in I regretted jumping in because it made me feel the way I felt when we landed and we crashed. I'm shocked that it's freezing still, but I'm also shocked that it didn't bother him. He just kept swimming. He's so determined. The look on his face was so determined to get our equipment back. He wasn't going to live like this anymore. He couldn't stand the people; he looked down on them so terribly bad. He could be very demeaning sometimes, listening to him go on and on about the people we were with. They had saved our lives, and he still felt like they were just animals. We dove and I went back up for air. And he didn't come up for a while. I thought he got caught on something. I needed to go down, so I sucked in my breath and I went down and pushed against the water and the cold and I start panicking thinking he's dead, he's definitely dead, he's stuck, he's stuck somewhere in the ship, and he's run out of breath. Then I see him swimming towards me with the red crystals. He has so many of them in his hands, and he hands some off to me and we propel up to the top together, holding them together so we don't drop them. And he has very big ones, very long ones about three to four inches wide, maybe five inches wide on some of the larger ones. And some of them are about ten to twelve inches long.

S: *What happens next?*

J: He is so happy. For the first time in months he's so happy because now he knows we can begin, and we can get the technology, and we can do it both ways. We can do it his way, and we can do it my way. And we can see who is the more successful one.

S: *So, he was planning on splitting from you then?*

J: I think he was planning on splitting from us the day that ship crashed. I convinced him to stay. He had wanted to go in one direction, and I had wanted to go in another, and I made my crew follow me, and that is when we found the humans.

S: *Could you tell me more about what you look like? And what he looks like?*

J: We actually are very similar looking. We all are from the same planet and we all have silvery blond hair and very tall bodies. We're not giants, but taller than most people. We're thinner and athletic looking. Our faces are longer than most people's faces that you see now, very elongated but with human qualities to them. Our heads are also slightly larger because our brains are larger. So our heads jut out a bit more; they're a bit rounder up top and a little bit wider. We all have the same eyes that look a bit cat-like and curled up. Most of us have light eyes but they will vary in color to what looks like purple, green, blue and light grey. We don't have brown eyes on our planet. That is something entirely human. We are very light-eyed. We have very deep furrowed brows on our foreheads. It's not a marking but very deep wrinkles, almost like a dimple but something that comes from eons of worrying.

S: *So, your society spent years worrying?*

J: I believe we were very worried about the continuation of our species, and after so many generations of worrying, it became a part of our physical nature, our physicality. We were very sure that our planet would not survive our species. And this took its toll on our physical bodies.

S: *That's why you came to Earth, correct?*

J: Yes, we were running out of resources and we knew we had to seed the planets.

S: *How is your planet now?*

J: It is still there. However, it looks like it no longer has people but vapor mists of energy of what was once people there. There are, however, still pyramids with big spires on top that hold our history.

S: *Where is that planet?*

J: Very far away and behind the Big Dipper.

S: *Where are all the people from that planet now?*

J: There are no people on that planet, just energy memories of our civilization. The people who left are here on this Earth, or they seeded other planets.

S: *Are a lot of people on this Earth from that planet?*

J: Yes, many. At first, we were some of the only ones.

S: *How did these people get here?*

J: In the beginning, it was as I arrived here in ships. Many of us had crash landed and once you have been here, in the afterlife you can choose again to stay here, or you can try something different. And after many generations you're not given the choice if you want to leave here.

S: *Why is that?*

J: You forget the choice. You get stuck here with the things you would like to do here. There is so much time, though, that there is no need to worry about that. It just takes a long period of time before some people can evolve past it and choose to leave Earth and go to other places for their next existences.

S: *So, could you tell me more about that other crew member that survived?*

J: I had tried for so long to convince him that there was a deep need for us to breed with the others that had taken us in, and to continue our mission, and he did not agree with me. Even though I tried and I tried, and had taken a mate and we had tried for children and failed so many times...and every time there was never a comforting word from him, it was always the same look. This look I would get of telling me you're doomed, you're doomed, you will never succeed, you're doomed. And one day he was gone.

S: *Where did he go?*

J: He jumped into a chasm. He found a way to create a chasm, and he took the technology we had from the ship. He took most of the technology we were able to salvage after our ship crashed, and he took that with him and when he came out the other side of the chasm, he was on what we would call the island of Atlantis now. And that was where he began his journey.

S: *Could you explain what it means to go through a chasm?*

J: It is like an elevator that transports you to different places on this planet, and the right people can use it.

S: *How can they use it?*

J: There are elements that need to be combined. You would need water, wind and sound, and it has to line up properly with the stars because there is a light that has to come down from them that will help open it up. He was building this using some of our technology behind my back. I had told him that there was no need for the chasms, that we had found humans, and that we were fine where we were. Also, if we risked going into the chasm, there was no way of knowing where we would end up. You can't direct yourself in the chasm.

S: *You can't direct yourself?*

J: The chasm will send you where you need to go. It does not allow you to pick where you want to go, so I feared we would never return had we jumped into the chasm. He went anyway and when he did, he took the technology with him.

S: *What type of technology did he take with him?*

J: The technology that could melt stones and a few other devices that allowed the generation of electricity. When he arrived at this new place, that some would call Atlantis, he found a new group of primitive humans, and he did not breed with them. Instead he educated them and used the technology to begin to turn their minds differently.

S: *How did he do that?*

J: With our technology he became a God to them. He was able to do things that they did not understand.

S: *What could he do?*

J: He could take stones and levitate them and with these lasers, he could cut them and create these stone structures and palaces, or what would become palaces, sometimes it would take a long time to finish these structures. But he began to use the primitive humans in ways, almost like slave labor, and used the fear and the creation of religion to control them. **That was the beginnings of Atlantis.** Their alien origins and their technology all come from a very emotionally cold place of discovery and manipulation. When he arrived and started what was known as Atlantis, the beginning was very tumultuous. He was like a mad man playing mad scientist creating an army of people in his own image by genetically modifying these humans that had been free on that island for many generations. He would corral them, imprison them, turning them into his servants, changing them and their wills to do what he wanted. In the beginning, it was very rough and rudimentary, but he was soon able to get many of these new trained workers to begin building his city. He used so much equipment there. There was a lot of early machinery that was used. He had the enslaved humans digging the canals, the roads around his capital that he created. There was so much stone carving and he just continues to add and add to his labor force. It looked like he had almost an army of them by the time he died.

S: *What happened after he died?*

J: The humans had been so brainwashed and so changed that they continued this. They continued the patterns and the building, they did not know anything except that now. They had a new leader who was hand-picked by the old leader **because the old leader believed that power should be isolated. It should not be spread out. He believed that people cannot do the right thing when given power; they only do the right thing when one person has power. He believed that the most beneficial way to have a society was to remove choice from the society, and that he felt would allow for an easier flow to success.**

S: *What about the origins of your people?* **The origins of Lymuria?**

J: The origins of my people come from love and the need for something to be passed down and the creation of equality amongst people, the continuation of the original plan that we were sent to do.

S: *What was the original plan?*

J: To seed this Earth, to come here, to begin the next civilizations of a better race of people.

S: *Was it planned to have these civilizations of Atlantis and Lymuria become separate?*

J: I know from where I have been that the plan all along was to have us crash land there and to see what would happen as a result. I didn't know how things would unfold. But it was intentional that we should be here and that we should be doing this. The rest is left up to the unfolding of life and the decisions that we made while we were here. So yes, there was destiny, and there was also human decision that factored in.

In the months that followed this session with Jen, I started receiving other clients who recounted similar lifetimes as these other worldly beings. Many described the same silvery long hair, cat-shaped eyes and even the same blue jumpsuits. Provided below is part of a session with a client named Christelle that I did two months after the session with Jen detailed above. Christelle had described during her regression one thing that differed from Jen's description of the jumpsuit, the badge they each had located on their chest. Jen described hers as a badge for planetary exploration, but Christelle saw a bolt that she felt was associated with her work collecting samples on Earth. I believe this begins to show the amount of effort and different assignments that were dispersed during the earliest days of the genesis of our species. This is Christelle's session:

S: *What do you become aware of?*
C: I see grass, and trees, and I'm holding some mushrooms.
S: *What else do you notice there?*
C: I'm in a forest. It's beautiful. Everything is lush. I'm in Washington or Oregon.
S: *Look down at your body. Do you have feet there?*
C: Yes, I have black boots on. These boots are very flexible; I can run very fast in them.
S: *Look up the body. What are you wearing on the rest of your body?*
C: I'm wearing my suit, it's a body suit, it's tight, it's for work.
S: *What color is this suit? Tell me more about it.*
C: It's blue and has a design on the front of it.
S: *What does this design look like?*
C: It is a bolt, like a lightning bolt.
S: *What do you look like?*
C: I have pale skin and pale eyes and my hair is a silvery white that runs down the back of my shoulders.
S: *What type of work do you do?*
C: Well right now I'm visiting and I'm enjoying just visiting here. I visit a lot because it's so beautiful...but for work I collect samples. I collect leaves and rocks and soil samples.
S: *What do you do with them?*
C: I take them back to the ship or to our planet to see if everything is going according to plan. If the samples are good, then that means the Earth is doing what it needs to do. If the samples are bad, then it means that things are not good.
S: *What do you have collected today?*
C: I have three different types of mushrooms and I have three different vials of soil from three different parts of the forest, and I have some from the water. I'm by the beach as well, this beach has black sand.
S: *Do you see any animals there?*
C: I haven't seen too many, just one fox. It was a white fox. We just looked at each other. We don't take anything from animals.
S: *You don't take anything from animals?*
C: No, and we never harm anything. Even the leaves and the soil samples and mushrooms, we ask if it's OK to take them with us.
S: *Who do you ask?*
C: We ask them! We ask the species of plants, and we ask the Earth if it's OK.

S: How do you ask this?
C: Oh telepathically, mostly they say yes, but sometimes they don't agree, so then we wouldn't take them. Everything has it's own set of consciousness.
S: How does the Earth feel about what you are doing?
C: The Earth is part of what we're doing. There is a collective that set up the Earth. The Earth is a perfect situation for human beings to live on.
S: Who set up the Earth?
C: Well we all did, the Collective did. We wanted to breed humans.
S: You wanted to breed humans? What was the purpose of that?
C: Humans are the experiment. We wanted to see what they will do. They are the perfect consciousness for the material plane because they can enjoy everything about this Earth. We don't enjoy the same types of things, the pleasures of the flesh, because we are a higher consciousness. We also don't have access to those things. Many of us incarnate into a human body to experience this or share parallel lives with humans or even parallel consciousness, but once we are in the higher consciousness, we don't have access to that level of visceral experiences.
S: Where do you come from?
C: Where I come from we live together in communities that are conscious, and we have families. It's different in that no one claims one another. We come together as we choose. It's blissful always.
S: Do you have a family?
C: I do. They are beautiful light beings; they are all very highly intelligent and magnetic.
S: What do you enjoy the most about where you live?
C: Joining together the energies and communing together.
S: How were the samples that you collected today?
C: I am not the one who inspects them. I am just the collector, but I hand the samples off to someone else that looks like me.
S: Does everyone have the same lightning bolt?
C: Yes, that is our uniform when we come to Earth.
S: Does it mean anything? This lightning bolt?
C: It means inspiration. We only have our bodies when we come to Earth. And we only look like this when we come here on the off chance that we are seen, so that we won't scare anyone. We are very energetically different though, and our auras are very inviting.
S: On this day that you are collecting samples, what else are you doing?
C: I'm going to stay in the woods for a while. Time is different for us. Time is a human concept. I might be there for what you would call two weeks but for me it would be five seconds. I could glean what I need from the forest in milliseconds, but for humans it might feel like a long time. Time is not linear at all; it is subjective.
S: What did the Earth look like when you first started coming down to it?
C: It was lush and beautiful, mostly covered with water, but the atmosphere was perfect for the type of being we were going to create. When we first started coming, it was difficult.
S: Tell me more. Why was it difficult?

As I was delving into this session, compelling information about Antarctica emerged. It is interesting to note that this was not my only client to bring up the ice-laden land of Antarctica in connection to earlier beings on Earth. From what has been shared from the Subconscious, it paints the continent as an early outpost for human creation.

C: Well, it didn't start out as difficult, and I was not there at this time. But when we first started the project, we settled into what would be called Antarctica now. It used to be very green there and very sunny.

S: *It used to be green in Antarctica?*

C: Yes, there were fields of green, not many trees, and it was very rocky around the borders of it. There were many geodesic domes all around that we put into a pattern. From above you would see they are in an order that would look like a flower.

S: *What are these domes?*

C: They are homes to plants or other things we were growing…the humans…the animals…everything that we were working on and perfecting for our later stay on Earth. The domes look metallic almost.

S: *What did your people look like then? Did they always look the same?*

C: Similar. We have always had that very pale look with silvery blond hair and the vivid colored eyes, although back then we were lankier and more elongated.

S: *When your people came to Earth, did they experience things differently from when they were on their home planet?*

C: Yes. When you come to Earth you transition into the atmosphere here, and you experience what humans experience, like hunger and emotions. At first, it was very happy there and promising because there was so much joy in the work as they all knew what they were starting. They are starting this new world. **The world hadn't been touched yet by all the negativity that will come there.** It used to feel there like a beautiful summer's day out on a green field of grass with a blue sky above, a very fresh and happy place.

S: *What happened?*

C: Everything almost had to be shut down. The experiment was almost scrapped.

S: *Why?*

C: It had gone in the wrong direction. There were things that snuck in, almost looks like it attached to one of our ships or landed here on an asteroid, but it interfered with the project and the results. There was disease that was brought unintentionally through this.

S: *It had snuck here?*

C: Yes, it had hightailed it on the back of something coming here. It had a consciousness that affected the physicality of the people that came there. The first beings settling Antarctica fell into a depression because of it. They didn't understand what it was and what was going on with their bodies when they would fall ill. And the misery that it brings to them is what unfurls this whole web of negativity that begins to spread, and it affects their work. It affects the things that they are growing.

S: *Why did it almost get shut down?*

C: Because **this was not the experiment that they had intended. It was almost completely destroyed, but the experiment had already started spreading on its own accord. This was the only reason they did not scrap the entire experiment.** Life had found a way despite all of this. Life had evolved on its own and this was something they did not expect.

S: *So, what happened to those beings?*

C: They could not destroy the new growing life when they saw that it had a consciousness to it, so they decided to shut down their version of the experiment, what they had grown. And they distributed this new growing life to different places. When they built the chasms, they brought people that they had genetically modified, and the other things that they had grown, and they distributed them into different places and kept track of them from afar. Time works differently when you go through this wormhole that brings you here from the home planet. Thousands and thousands of years can pass here on Earth, but it passes much faster for people on the home planet. So, thousands of years can pass, and you can continuously go through the wormhole to check on the evolution and see what is going on. When they realized that there were positive results to this and that we still needed Earth as a backup planet, we continued the experiment. We all felt a sense of relief. We had proven the case of continuing Earth with the natural evolution that happened when we left the experiment and closed the Antarctica laboratory down.

S: *What happened to Antarctic itself? Why is it covered by ice?*

C: In the shifting of poles, the shifting of climate, and the freezing of lands, Antarctica was covered by ice miles deep.

S: *What would you find if you could dig miles deep under the ice in Antarctica now?*

C: You would find evidence of the original colonies who seeded this planet. You would find many keys that would link our heritage to somewhere beyond this planet.

S: *What type of keys would you find?*

C: You would find ancient technology such as the ability to form stones into shapes very quickly, the ability to lift and magnetize things without needing a crane, and cooking technology to cook and keep food for long periods of time. However, you would also find microscopic diseases, so Antarctica is better left alone.

S: *Has anyone ever found any of this evidence?*

C: There have been many explorations that have gone and studied and found many unexplainable things that they are not allowed to let people know.

S: *What did they find?*

C: They have found different types of metals in ice-cored drills, miles deep into the Earth. The findings would lead to the understanding that there were, in fact, more advanced ancient civilizations before ours.

I believe there is much more to the continent of Antarctica than we have understood as a society. This information from the Subconscious leaves me with many more questions than answers, and perhaps it is best left for another book, as I feel it is a can of worms too immense to begin to open, just yet.

CHAPTER 4: THE CHILDHOOD OF PRINCESS KALA

Until now, Jen and I had been receiving information about her extra-terrestrial lifetime, yet we still had not received much information about the lifetime we thought we were supposed to uncover until finally in May of 2019, we were shown her childhood. It was a few days after this session that Jen had told me that her name in that lifetime was Kala, a piece of information that had arrived one morning while waking from sleep. We learned later that this name meant princess in the Lymurian language. This is the story and the ancient history of Princess Kala and her beautiful childhood in Amun.

S: Let's drift and float to a memory of when you were a child in the land that people call Lymuria. Be there now. What do you become aware of?
J: There are beautiful gardens surrounding me that have a beautiful waterfall that kind of just cascades down. The waterfall comes out over a stone lever and just falls down like a sheet of water into the middle of the gardens. This garden has lots of lush and tropical looking flowers. It is very colorful with reds, purples, oranges and yellows all dotted throughout. The waterfall is part of the water system that they have inside the palace, and this water is fed into it. There are also very colorful fish in the pool that the waterfall flows into.
S: Are there any smells associated with that place?
J: It has a smell of heavy water and jasmine scent. There are very beautiful birds around that look like white peacocks with red and yellow tips on the end. They are very elegant looking birds that look like they have long feathered hats on almost.
S: Can you hear them? Is there any sound there?
J: Yes. They make a very strange "Ah" sound when they talk to one another. These are very well-maintained courtyard gardens that are inside the palace. They are in and around this palace.
S: What does the palace look like?
J: I see my favorite places to go. I can see my balcony and the water that is nearby. The entrance to the palace is shaped like an A pattern, without the line through the middle. The stone was cut that way. The entrance is very big. It goes down first before you go up into the palace to keep the cooling mechanism working. This helps to cool the building. When you get inside it, the air feels very light. There is stone all around it; it's like a limestone with a bit of wear and black markings on it where mold has grown over the years. It's very old, white stone. I see that there are very large wide columns all around the building that are very smooth and have these cups on the tops of them that hold everything up.
S: Who made these? Do you know?
J: They were all made early on by the early colonists from the home planet that brought the technology with them. Within the first couple of hundred years of their colonization they made the majority of these structures.
S: Were they built by humans? The colonists were not human?
J: They were built by extraterrestrials and their descendants, who were the humans mixed with extraterrestrial genes. Within the first five to six hundred years of their arrival here on

Earth, these things were built.

S: *Look down at your feet. What do your feet look like there?*

J: They are small and brown with very white toenails.

S: *Are you wearing anything on your body?*

J: A tan colored leather sash that goes down from my shoulder and crosses my body and a skirt that goes down to my knees. It is made out of something that looks like leather but in a raised pattern that looks like a leaf's veins.

S: *How do you wear your hair?*

J: My hair is just pulled back and tied at the nape of my neck and broken into two separate braids from there, one for each side.

S: *What are you doing today?*

J: I'm going down to **the Labyrinth** with my grandmother. We go through this stone doorway and down this wide set of steps that go down a hillside leading eventually down to the water. Before we get to the water, there is a platform with a large stone-made labyrinth that goes up to your knee. There are a lot of conch shells around this labyrinth that look like they're all standing up trying to catch the wind in them. They've all had the tops cut off of them so that you can hear the sound of the wind as it hits them. It's very windy in this area. There is a natural vortex created in the way that this is built and the way the wind comes off the ocean when it hits the shells. When the sound hits the conch shells while you are walking the labyrinth and trying to figure out an answer to a question, the answer will vibrationally come to you.

S: *How does this work?*

J: It changes your frequency, your vibration, and it opens up the path to the answer that is trying to get to you.

S: *The answer is trying to get to you? And this opens the path for it to get there?*

J: Yes, as long as you are wandering through the labyrinth while meditating over your question, it will allow for the opening to the answer to take place.

S: *Anything else that seems interesting about this?*

J: On the days that we walk down to the labyrinth, my grandmother would tell me **the legend, the prophecy of the two sisters.**

S: *Could you tell me this legend?*

J: It is the legend of the two sisters, the prophecy we are all told when we are young about two sisters being separated who are destined to be reunited one day. My grandmother would tell me that a mother and her two daughters were walking one day when an earthquake began to shake the island. There was a rock that was about to fall on one of the daughters while they were walking next to a chasm. The mother saw this happening and before it fell and killed the child, the mother pushed her child into the chasm in order to push her out of harm's way, but the chasm activated and pulled her child in. Before this child had fallen into the chasm, she had always felt like she was second best to her other sister, always in her shadow. She didn't feel as good or as valuable as her sister. And when her mother pushed her and she arrived through the chasm into a new part of the world, she found the importance that she was seeking there. But she cannot get back to her family, to her sister. The legend is that they will reunite one day and that there is another civilization out there in a different part of the world. The reunion of these sisters will result in the connecting of these two civilizations. As I see this from my perspective now, I see that this prophecy was meant to be misconstrued in later generations. It almost cloaks Atlantis because my people believed that the Atlanteans were the people in that story that we were supposed to reunite with, when in actuality, the sister that was pushed into the chasm arrived inside Mt. Shasta, California and was greeted by a group of loving colonists, the original ones that lived there. We did not know of the people in Atlantis, even though the people in Atlantis were the true prophecy. There was a discrepancy in the legend that looks like it was intentional.

S: *Did the sisters ever reunite?*

J: Only in the afterlife. The legend was meant to serve as the bridge to bring these two civilizations, Atlantis and Lymuria together.

S: *Let's move to another important day when you were a child in that lifetime in Lymuria. Be there now. What do you notice?*

J: I'm on these steps that are made out of white stone and they're cut very specifically and geometrically. There are lots of steps going down into this well at the bottom. It goes down very deep, maybe one hundred feet down, and the steps zigzag down.

S: *The steps zigzag down?*

J: Yes, they zigzag in a pattern down the sides of this well. It's rectangular in form, and at the bottom there is a pool of water that fills when the rainy months come. At the bottom is a little boy about my age with his mother.

S: *What does he look like?*

J: He has very thick dark, straight hair that goes down past his ears. He has it parted on the side and it kind of goes over his eye a little bit. He sticks one side behind the other ear and he's very tiny and bony, but he is athletically built and strong looking as well, not sickly looking. He sees me, and as he does, he can see that I'm about to fall because I'm not paying attention where I'm going. He yells out to warn me to stop and to look, but it is too late. I fall and he breaks my fall. This fall leaves him with a small scar on his forehead that always reminds me in later years that he saved my life.

S: *He saved your life?*

J: I think I would've been very hurt by the fall, or possibly worse. My older sister had died in that well by falling and breaking her neck when she was three years old. My mother had never shared that with me. One day I heard one of my caregivers talking about it.

S: *No one told you about this?*

J: My grandmother finally did after I confronted her, but my mother never talked about her first child. I believe my mother was possibly less affectionate towards me as a result of this tragedy, out of fear of getting too close to another child again.

S: *Tell me more about this boy?*

J: We have a friendship and bond that begins there, and we often carefully walk to the bottom and play in the water. I show him a trick that I can do with my mind.

S: *What can you do?*

J: It's a trick where I can take a stick and make the stick turn into a snake. He doesn't like snakes and I play this joke on him. I do this for years. I turn sticks into snakes in front of his eyes. He absolutely hates snakes as there were a lot of snakes where he lives, but I don't have a lot where I live, which is in the palace.

S: *Where does he live?*

J: He lives close by. He comes over quite often to play because his father is one of my guards and they also trust his mother. So, he is allowed to come and play and to keep me company.

S: *Tell me more.*

J: He would go to a school while I would do my studies in the palace, but after we were done, we would meet up in the late afternoons, early evenings, when the school would let out. We would swim a lot and he would catch things with his hands.

S: *What could he catch?*

J: Little long, silver fish with a red streak on the top of them.

S: *What else did you play as a child?*

J: He would bring this game with him. It looked like an old version of backgammon with little stones that were polished and you would jump them on this board that was made from stone. The purpose was to get rid of all of your stones. We would play this game, but we would also run around the gardens.

S: *Tell me more about the gardens?*

J: My mother's gardens looked like the Garden of Eden. These gardens were within and outside of the palace and out into the public sphere. There were many of them, but the most important ones she kept close to the palace. Some of the plants were from the same seeds of the plants that had been brought over from another planet. These were the special ones that were grown within the palace's gardens. They were not the original trees, but they were the descendants and were continuously planted so they were still the same.

S: *Do you get a sense of what they looked like, or what they were?*

J: One looks like a lychee. It has the same aromatic flavor to it where you taste it and it tastes almost like a jasmine flower or a rose, a sweet, heavy flavor.

S: *Were there any benefits of these fruits for the human body?*

J: The flavoring and nourishment was the taste of home. That was the most important, the nostalgia it would bring to those who were colonizing from a different planet. They would have things that were familiar that they could use as a mental boost of nostalgia.

S: *They remember their home?*

J: Some of us could vaguely remember our past lives as earlier colonists that came and seeded around the Earth and it became a tradition for us to have those fruits. The colonists brought certain plants and seeds with them on certain missions that they felt would help them in the future trigger memories and help their hybridization experiment prosper.

S: *Are there any plants that look interesting to you?*

J: Something else that looks like ginger with bulbs in the ground that grows in watery places. They have very thick stems that shoot up straight out of the bulbs in swampy water. This plant was used as a pain relief by macerating the bulb enough to be chewed and that would reduce pain and inflammation, but it also could be boiled and eaten and it would dull your pain that way as well. It isn't around today. Some of the last of it was growing when our island was destroyed.

S: I see. Is there anything else about your childhood that you notice, or that seems interesting?
J: I see marketplaces that are covered by canopies all throughout long walkways. There are just piles of spices. It looks like nuts and fruits piled up very high around where you walk. It's like an eight-foot-wide pathway through this place and it's all separated. And it smells very good, like cinnamon and something that smells like pumpkin spice, spicy but sweet. There are people stopping to look at us and bringing us offerings of their things to try. Delicious little things that they have made. Treats, and things like that.
S: Why do they do that?
J: It looks like they want to please me, and they want me to talk to others about their treats, like a bragging right kind of a thing. They want me to prefer theirs to the others' treats. It kind of reminds me of what Halloween is like now, just going around with my young friend to these places, and each place gives us something delicious. And not being able to eat dinner after this is over. And us just enjoying ourselves and hoarding these things back at the palace.
S: What else do you notice?
J: This whole community looks very serene, peaceful, and kind.
S: Do you get a sense of why it's so peaceful there, and why people are so kind?
J: There is very little to worry about because of the lack of sickness and because of our immunity to most sicknesses. There is also such an abundance of food and things that grow and nourish people there that there is very little to worry about. The basic needs are being met and then some, and because of that, it produces a calmer person who is more logical and open to educating themselves.
S: Is there anything about the education that seems interesting?
J: It looks like there are many ways to be educated there. There isn't one particular method for each person. Education was like a multifaceted thing where you would really go into what you were adept in, but everyone received the same education in a couple of areas. Everyone learned how to read and write our language. Everyone also learned about the basics of astronomy so that they could maneuver themselves around.
S: What do you mean by that, maneuver themselves around?
J: You could travel at night using the stars to guide you around our island. The stars were the guiding posts for this type of travel, and the people would mostly travel by boat at night in order to do this.
S: What if it was cloudy at night?
J: Then there wouldn't be travel for the evening because this was our guiding system.
S: Would people travel during the day?
J: They would travel during the day using our road system to go from place to place, but there was a heavy element of astronomy education and watching the stars. The equinox was also very important to us.
S: **Why was the equinox so important?**
J: The power of the day and the night equaling would make the ability for the chasms to naturally open.
S: What happens when the chasm opens?
J: You could transport yourself into a new place on the Earth.

S: Would people do that?

J: Not regularly, but over the course of history this would be done many times.

S: Did your culture know where the chasms were?

J: Yes, the biggest one of these chasms was located on the outskirts of our island on what is called Easter Island now. The Maori stone heads were originally placed in a circle and made into a chasm. When the wave occurred many of them were dislodged and sent all over the island and buried into the land.

S: Were there any other times when the chasm would open?

J: It could be done manually if the right amount of crystals were placed in the right positions with the right type of equipment. It was like a fail-safe that was programmed in when the chasm was created by the earliest visitors to this planet. If the crystals were not available or if the technology wasn't available, there were at least two days a year that you could access the chasm and transport yourself.

S: Where exactly could you go within the chasm?

J: The chasms were made to transport you along the lay lines, or energy centers to other locations on the Earth. However, when you would travel you would never know where you would end up.

CHAPTER 5: KALA'S TEENAGE YEARS IN LYMURIA/AMUN

As the months progressed, Jen and I traveled past the childhood of Kala and entered into her teen years. During this part of her past life regression she was able to describe in detail the palace she lived in and the advancements that could be found in this long forgotten ancient empire.

S: What do you become aware of?

J: The water, the crystal-clear water.

S: Look down at your feet and tell me what you have on your feet?

J: I can't see my feet because they're in the water, but I can feel that they are very hardened feet standing on smooth pebbles.

S: Look up your body and tell me what you have on your body?

J: I have a wrap on. It's a brownish green wrap made of plants and animal skin, and the top matches the bottom.

S: Do you have any jewelry on?

J: Rings and bracelets that seem to be made of a gold and leather material.

S: What does your face look like?

J: It is ruddy brown skin with a slight red glow to it. It's very healthy looking. My hair is very dark, frizzy and curly. Sometimes it could be braided back during training. My eyes, they seem like they're a bit saucer-shaped, wider, black-brown.

S: What about your nose?

J: Very flat and wide and my jaw is wider, and I have full lips. I feel as if I'm sixteen or seventeen.

S: Do you get a sense of what you're doing there?

J: I get a sense that the ocean is warning me about what's coming, and that I have to stay on my toes as I'm soon to be leader here.

S: Do you get a sense of what is to come?

J: No. Well, maybe somewhere in the back of my mind I have seen it.

S: Tell me more about that?

J: My grandmother used to show me how to communicate with the dead. I saw it there.

S: How did you see it? Could you tell me more?

J: We would stare at each other's faces using a certain crystal until we would start to see visions and communicate with another realm. Once we looked into the future, and all we saw was water. It scared us, and we never brought it up again. We never looked into the future after that, but I always had a sense that something was coming. I think I always had a nagging feeling that something was going to go wrong. My grandmother always told me to push that away.

S: Were you able to push that away?

J: No, and I think I lived with that in the back of my mind. It seems to be like a dark cloud always hanging over my head.

S: Tell me more about your life there. Where do you live now as a teenager?

J: I still live in the palace. It's very private and secluded where only certain people can go. The sea is very calm in front of us, almost like a bay, like an area that has a very low tumble to the surf.

S: *How do you feel here?*

J: It's very calming.

S: *Is there anyone else there with you?*

J: No, I'm alone with cold stone walls behind me. There's another doorway that leads into my bedroom.

S: *What does the doorway look like?*

J: It looks like it has been cut from stone that has been molded together. And it is a very thick stone passage, but there's no door to it, just an opening that you walk into.

S: *What does your bedroom look like?*

J: Seems like there is a circular mat in the middle of the room which is where I sleep.

S: *What does this mat look like it's made of?*

J: It's a soft covering. It's stuffed with some type of cushioning, like animal hair, but not feathers. Some type of sheep, that kind of material, just fluffed into it.

S: *How does it feel to sleep on this?*

J: Feels very comfortable and it's relaxing because there's a gentle breeze that comes in constantly and cools me off. And it keeps insects off of me as well. It seems like the mat is a little bit elevated on the platform that it sits on. There are light sources on the wall, but they're not made from an open flame or electricity.

S: *Tell me more about that?*

J: They're like a soft glowing sconce with an orange glow coming from them.

S: *Do you get a sense of what they're made of?*

J: It looks like they are covered by glass. They've somehow used a series of reflections from a bigger light source that looks like piping and mirrors that project this glow to illuminate these glass orbs on the sconces.

S: *Tell me more.*

J: They were built into the room long before me and my time, and it looks like the lights are just as much a part of the building as the blocks are. The actual building itself has a strange history to it.

S: *Tell me more about this history.*

J: There was a story that goes back to our earlier ancestors who used what was left of their technology. They built this palace to begin the civilization that they were meant to begin.

S: *Could you tell me more about that history?*

J: It is something my grandmother would tell me to make me go to sleep. I remember that as she would tell me this, I would trace the lines that connected the rock with my fingers, and I remember her explaining that it was made using something like a crystal laser. It could burn off a piece of the rock very quickly and fit it together precisely so we would have a tight fortress.

S: *Does your culture still have this crystal laser technology?*

J: No, that was something we had and then lost early on. The building itself was very impressive.

S: What do you mean by that?

J: How it would retain it's coolness on the hotter months inside so that the further into the building you go, the cooler it would be.

S: Is there anything else interesting about the building that you can tell me?

J: They had a system of running water that was gravity fed that would run throughout the palace, so there would be certain areas you could go to have fresh water to drink or to bathe or wash with. You could empty your water back into that, and it would flush out. I think this pavilion that I see outside was just for me. Now I remember, that was my area.

S: It was just for you?

J: It was just for me. My helpers did not go there. I had a nanny who would take care of me. She took an oath to care for me and was always there for me as she had no other family. My basic needs were met by her. My grandmother was very busy but also had time for me because she felt that if that time wasn't spent with me, then I wouldn't be prepared for the role ahead of me. She would tell me stories and anecdotes and experiences of hers from when she was ruling to explain to me how I could be the best version of myself when I ruled next.

S: Were there any stories that stood out as important?

J: Yes, she dealt with a famine in her early years, and she received a message in her dreams explaining the purpose of the famine. The dream explained how to redo irrigation ditches. It had something to do with not enough water, but she found the answer through a series of meditations.

S: Is this different, or the same, as the meditations you were describing?

J: These are the same, and my grandmother started to spend more time with me to cheer me up.

S: Why did you need cheering up?

J: My friend and I got into trouble and he was sent away to go train.

S: Why did he get sent away?

J: I did not see it coming, the feelings that we were each developing for one another. One day we were play fighting and all of a sudden, he pushed me to the ground by accident and we fell into each other's arms. I had never felt that feeling, that bolt of energy before and we locked eyes and kissed for a moment and unfortunately, we were not alone. After that, it was not considered appropriate for us to be together. It was very sad for the both of us. They felt that we were getting too close and my decisions were being influenced by him and that was not how my training should be. My decisions should be influenced by the women who ruled before me, not the son of a guard. That is what my mother's belief was. My grandmother agreed with her and so he was sent away to be trained mentally, physically, and spiritually by a brotherhood **called the Nacaal Brotherhood who were the keepers of our history and of our stories.**

S: So, he was trained by them?

J: Yes.

S: Could you tell me more about that group? What do they do?

J: They would do similar things to what Buddhist monks do now; they would fast and pray. It was more of a meditation and less of a prayer than it is now. It was an ongoing effort to continuously keep records of our history and of our history of this experiment. This brotherhood dates back to the earliest days of the colony and was set up by those who crash landed. They were the descendants of those earliest people, the record keepers and they were mostly men. There were certain women who decided to join, but it has historically been more of the men who volunteer for this role because it is a life of solitude. They cannot marry and they cannot have families.

S: Where do they keep these records?

J: They have a large circular, colosseum type stone structure that they keep a lot of the records in. And in front of the structure there is a large brass bell that has one large cup on top of another large cup. It's almost like a honeycomb, one on top of the other, larger and larger, and larger, almost like a Christmas tree in formation. It's very big in front, about forty feet up into the air. The large bell was also a way to communicate with other parts of our territory because it acted as a communication device. However, all these records that were stored there are now in fragments that are very well hidden away in a part of Egypt and covered by sand. Some fragments have found their way to areas within Mt. Shasta, California, but they are very corroded, and things have started to grow on top of them, like crystals or a calciferous growth. There are also still some fragments in northern coastal Asia, and also in India are copies of something that would have been in these records.

S: Are there any good copies?

J: No, the copies are not very good. There is a lot lost in translation.

S: How did they get copies into India?

J: When the cataclysm happened and those who had been spared their lives were traveling to find new homes, a lot of the legends came with these survivors. Over time the information was bastardized and changed. Little bits of the information here and there were tweaked and changed to the way people wanted it to be in that time.

S: When you scan the records of your people, what do you find the most interesting or important about those records?

J: They tell the story of our origins and of our rulers and how they overcame problems such as floods and droughts and swarms. The usual issues that people face. The most important thing was the divine bloodline that continues and what they called the **Gift of the Stars** which was our right to rule because our ancestors foresaw this need for our existence. This is the RH negative blood.

S: Could you tell me what the purpose of this bloodline is?

J: This is a very specific bloodline that is the result of the union and the success of that one child being born. It is a symbol of that union and the success of that. The O bloodline goes back to this as well. The O bloodline came from the mother and the RH factor came from the father. The father was the Commander and the first women that he mated with was the mother. The other bloodlines you see now are from different people from different planets that have come here to colonize.

S: Thank you very much. Is there anything else that looks interesting or important?

J: Today is a very beautiful day and I'm getting ready to train.

S: Tell me about this training.

J: The training is done in the morning. In this training I work with a long metal pole learning different kinds of swift movements. It was wooden at first, and then I moved up to using metal. This is just for practice and to learn self-defense. I train on a very small beach about ten feet from the end of the pavilion. The water just seems so calm.

S: *Is it always this calm?*

J: Sometimes it will get kicked up a little more, but it's usually very calm over there. I feel like it faces a protected bay area. I love my balcony and my place to be alone because I don't get a lot of time alone. This is the place I go to escape what is expected of me, and it's private. It's beautiful, and it was my mother's room before me, and my grandmother's room before her, and so on, and it will be my daughter's room in a few years.

S: *Do you have a daughter?*

J: In a few more years I will when I am around twenty.

CHAPTER 6: CHILDBIRTH IN LYMURIA/AMUN

I was interested to find out more about what it was like to give birth during that time in Lymuria, especially what it was like for a princess. I regressed Jen back to the day she gave birth to her daughter and found a truly joyful experience from that lifetime.

S: Let's leave that scene and move ahead in time to where you are having your daughter and be there now.
J: We're in the same room and they've given me something that puts me almost in a trance like state. It helps with the pain.
S: Tell me more about what they've given you?
J: It's a liquid and it's made from leaves, some type of leaf from a tree that has a bit of whiteness to it. They grind it down and make a paste out of it and then you smell it. When you breathe it in, it removes you from your body and removes you from the pain.
S: How does it feel after you breathe this in?
J: It gives you the feeling that you're slightly above your own body, just floating above it. A feeling that you're just slightly above the pain. You're aware of what's going on but your consciousness that feels the pain is floating slightly above you. Your physical body has been separated from the pain even though it's going through the movements.
S: Do you get a sense of what this plant is called?
J: It's a green leaf that is shaped like a long oval about the size of your forearm and it has a white waxy residue on it. They use a mortar and pestle to grind it up and make the paste before you breathe it in. You can't eat it, or it will poison you. There is a fire that's placed next to you so that the steam helps you breathe this in.
S: Who gives this to you?
J: The women that come to help deliver the babies. We have a lot of pain remedies from nature around us.
S: What other pain remedies would they use?
J: A lot of bark from trees for basic things, seems like everything has a double purpose. They were very knowledgeable about what did what.
S: How do they know these things?
J: There had been some basic training and understanding from the beginning of what would work when people started to come to this planet in order to help people in their new environment. Then trial and error over the years had allowed it to be perfected.
S: Who was in the room when you gave birth?
J: My mother, my grandmother, my nanny/ chamber maid, the medicine women, and the women who delivers the baby.
S: Tell me about the birth?
J: There was something strange going on in the sky that night.
S: Tell me about it.
J: It was just lightning and lightning and thunder with no rain and people said it was a good omen. Some people said it was a bad omen. No one could understand what it truly was

because they'd never seen anything like it. But it was thick. The pressure from the storm was very thick around us.

S: It was lightning without rain?

J: No rain. Just big clouds that piled in, lightning and thunder.

S: No one had ever seen something like that before?

J: Not how it had gathered the way it did with no rain that would come from it. It felt very humid and hot in the room because of it. I was sweating a lot...a lot.

S: What happened?

J: It took a little over a day and then she was born.

S: Tell me more about the birth.

J: She came out and she was so little. I thought she would've been bigger. She was screaming, wailing, and I remember them holding her up to me as they were presenting her, and they were so happy it was another girl. But everyone acted as if there was no other way. I wasn't so sure.

S: Did you think it could've been a boy?

J: I felt a lot of pressure that if it was a boy, that I would've broken what would have been thousands of years of a chain. Sometimes I thought that was what was wrong with me, that I would be the one to break that.

S: How do you feel now?

J: Ecstatic. She's covered with goo and blood and she's so loud. I'm so happy. My mother anointed her with an oil. It's a very fragrant oil sort of like a rose, but deeper than that. She rubbed this oil across her head, then they wrapped her up and patched me up.

S: How did they patch you up?

J: They took a cold compress while it was cold and had it mixed with some other ground up herbs. Then they placed it down below and wrapped me up in order to promote healing. They changed this every hour, and it was supposed to help contract the uterus and help stop the bleeding.

S: How did you feel when you first held your baby?

J: That she had always been there, that I couldn't remember ten minutes before when she wasn't there. She opened her eyes right away and looked at us, which they said was a great sign, to be born with your eyes wide open. And everyone was so excited that she was born, and she was alive. You could hear it throughout the palace. You could hear it all over the next few days; there were many celebrations.

S: What were they doing to celebrate?

J: They were enjoying themselves. They were drinking and eating. We had a type of fireworks that didn't have colors to it, but it had the same effect. I remember them setting them off and waking her up.

S: How did it make you feel that everyone was celebrating your baby?

J: I know I should've been very happy about it, but there was still something there that bothered me. Something that I couldn't shake off, just that cloud again, but I loved her. I absolutely loved her.

S: What did you enjoy doing with her?

J: I took her everywhere with me. They had a system of strapping the baby to you, and that's all I did. I had her with me so much that my mother at one point told me that I needed to allow others to take care of her.

S: How did that make you feel?

J: I disagreed with her because I told her that is not how I would like to be raised and if that's the way it had to be in the past then I was changing it. My baby would stay with me no matter what.

S: How did that feel when you told your mother this?

J: It was not a good moment for the two of us. She felt very differently about how a child should be raised, about how a future leader should be raised.

S: Did you continue to take her everywhere?

J: I did until she was about three years old, and then if I would go on any missions or any official duty, I started leaving her at the palace because...(gasp) I see why.

S: Why?

J: Because once they started arriving (the visitors) I didn't want her outside the palace. I wanted her protected. I didn't want her to be vulnerable. I left her in the care of a nanny and guards.

S: When the visitors started arriving, how did you feel about them?

J: I had a bad feeling. I was very confused as to why my people were so trusting of them in the beginning. My mother was very trusting of them.

S: Why was she so trusting of them?

J: Because of the legend, the prophecy. Her feeling was that they were distant relatives of ours and that this would be a time where we would merge our powers together for some type of fulfillment of destiny.

S: What about the visitors? Did they say what they wanted?

J: This is what they came to her with the premise of, and my mother felt that this is what was meant to happen in her reign. There were many tales about this.

S: What were the other tales?

J: There was another tale about how we knew we weren't the only ones out there. The information had been passed down that there had been others like us that had been sent to this planet. And we understood that humans had been sprinkled around what we knew as the world. We also had a good grasp of the fact that there was a spherical Earth too, that the Earth wasn't just this flat void. The astronomy aspect we understood well. We also understood that one day there was the possibility of us all being reunited or re-encountering each other for mutually beneficial growth.

S: If this was the prophecy and you and your mom knew about this legend, why did you have a bad feeling about them?

J: It just didn't seem right when I met them. I had a very bad, bad feeling when I met them.

S: How far away did they live from your civilization when you met them?

J: It would take probably months by boat to get to us. It was almost on the other side of the world. But they had found us. They had ways of transporting themselves in the air.

S: Were they more advanced in their technology?

J: Yes, and they seemed like they didn't just "find us," almost like they had been watching us for a while before presenting themselves. I always tried to point this out to my mother.

How do they know so much about us already if they just found us? Doesn't that strike you as a bit strange that they didn't come forward right away if they had the same prophecy as us?

S: Were these visitors men or women?

J: There was one central man and about five others that would travel with him. No women, only men, which wasn't very well received by us. They were mostly tall and all wearing black masks that covered their mouth and nose. The main one was very tall and very pale looking and had dark circles under his eyes. He must've been in his early fifties with stringy, greasy platinum blond hair. He just presented himself with such phoniness. I couldn't stomach him.

CHAPTER 7: THE VIRUS IN ATLANTIS AND THE MOTIVATION TO GO TO LYMURIA

I had questioned what the motivation was for the Atlanteans to go to Lymuria. The descriptions my clients provided made Atlantis seem very advanced. I wondered what they would want from a more primitive population?

S: Did the people in your group believe what the Atlanteans were saying?
J: There was a virus that was affecting the people of Atlantis and killing their people, and they claimed that they came to us for help.
S: Why did they decide to come to your island?
J: They had watched us for years and understood that we had a technology that created health for our people. We were immune to diseases and many viruses because of this technology.
S: Could you tell me about this technology?
J: It was a wave, an energy that we were able to tap into. Because of this, anyone in our company would be protected as well and immune to so many things. There were always many injuries, childbirth, and death, but there were very few illnesses on our continent because of this technology.
S: Tell me more.
J: This energy protects everything within the island up to the water's edge.
S: Do you get a sense as to why?
J: The energy just reflects off the water and bounces back in allowing it to be a solid circuit. Once you leave the island you lose it, and you can't give it to people. It's a gift that has to stay where it is.
S: So, was this what the Atlanteans were looking for?
J: Yes, there had been talk of our technology and it looks like it was a very top-secret project of the Atlanteans to come to our island and to come speak to us. I did not trust them, and my mother told me it was nonsense and my grandmother told me to stop looking so hard. But I saw the leader of that group for what he was, just an overgrown rat. Looking to trick people.
S: Why did you feel this way?
J: I saw these people taking to my mother about things, and it felt like they were talking double talk to her. She thought they were paying respect to her, but it feels as if they have absolutely no respect for her! They are very demeaning, but beneath the surface as to make it less obvious. I can't understand why she doesn't see that this is happening. They want to know about the red crystals that we have!
S: Tell me more about these red crystals. Where do they come from originally?
J: They were not crystals at first. They were these little seeds of energy that travel on things like asteroids or inside of suns that explode. I see explosions and big chunks of things being thrown all throughout the universes and they land in certain places. When it is the right place, it just begins to grow. We still understood how to use them from our earliest civilization here.
By using them, we can tap into communicating with our ancestors, and we can also use the

energy for many purposes such as our immunity. These crystals were hidden away by my mother the minute they asked about them. It was the smartest thing she did at that point. Something was triggered inside of her when they started asking about the red crystals. Once the visitors started asking about these, my grandmother and my mother went into a meditative state with the crystals to ask the Ancestors why these visitors from Atlantis wanted them and their message was an overwhelming warning to hide these. The red crystals are not to go near them. There's something about these red crystals that when they're used improperly, they can cause a massive explosion and allow for the civilization to begin again.

S: Like a reset button?

J: Yes, like a reset.

S: How many red crystals do you have?

J: We had several of them, and they held our history as well, information that helped us grow our civilization early on.

S: How do you get the information out of these crystals?

J: By touching them while you are in a meditative trance, but not everyone could receive the information?

S: Why not?

J: The lines had become diluted and those who did not have pure blood lines could get a basic idea, but they couldn't access all of the information inside of them like we could. We had a very clear connection because of our pure bloodlines.

S: Where were the red crystals hidden?

J: There was a natural cave on the top of a very tall mountain peak that jetted out to the ocean. It was very difficult to get to.

S: Who put them there?

J: My mother took them with some of her warriors, and they had to scale the mountain in order to make it to this cave. Then they took the crystals and arranged them in a certain way so that the sun and wind could hit them during the day and charge them. They were placed also in an area that didn't get too wet so as to not dull them. I've been there, and I remember there's a strange sound that the wind would make when it rolled through and charged them.

S: You could hear them charging? What did that sound like?

J: It was like a crackle, almost like when you hear water hitting electricity, but a very low hum, not loud. There would just be a slight crackle in the air to the point that the hairs on your arms would stand up. The crystals were hidden in this cave because we felt it was the most secluded place we could find based on our technology, and we felt that the Atlanteans would look within the palace for them. That is because we had created the impression that we would never separate ourselves from these crystals.

S: Why didn't they have any crystals like the ones you had? I thought the first leader of Atlantis brought red crystals with him when he entered the chasm?

J: They had only a few left. It was the one thing that they had lost over time and didn't realize what they had lost. They just had a very small one left. So, they knew about these crystals but didn't have enough of them to understand them.

CHAPTER 8: THE PEOPLE KEEP COMING

At first, it seemed like a coincidence when I started to notice more clients recounting lifetimes from Atlantis and Lymuria, but as the weeks progressed it seemed as if the Universe was plotting a way for this information to get to me. I began to recognize where my clients were as if I could even remember these places myself. Some of these clients had never read about these civilizations or heard anything other than myths about these places, yet clients were talking about these same islands, the same clothes, and the same way of life. In Jen's session her subconscious had mentioned that many people from this time period had reincarnated again and were walking the planet now, and that piece of information seemed more and more evident.

Olivia emailed me that she had wanted to try QHHT although she had never done anything like it before. Something in the back of her mind had been nagging her to do it. When we finally met, she acted very nervous and unsure if she could be hypnotized. Olivia came for a session not just out of curiosity but because she had had strange reoccurring dreams in which she was drowning. She also had a strange fear of the water that had made it impossible for her to swim. All her life she had lived with this distress and wanted desperately to enjoy the ocean, to swim, and to enjoy life to the fullest. This is what we found out during Olivia's session in August of 2019:

S: What do you become aware of?
O: The breeze. I can smell the breeze. It smells so beautiful...there are so many flowers here.
S: Tell me more about what you see around you.
O: Lots of flowers and plants. It looks like there are hills in the background, like rolling hills, and I'm close to a beach.
S: Tell me about the beach.
O: It's beautiful and calm, and it looks like the sand is made up of smooth pebbles.
S: Look down at your body and see if you have feet there?
O: I do. They look like women's feet; they're tan and I'm not wearing any shoes.
S: Look up the body now. Do you see what you're wearing?
O: Looks like some type of animal/ lizard skin. I'm wearing the bottom as a wrap and the top part is the same.
S: Do you have any jewelry on your body?
O: It looks like I have some gold bracelets. I have some roots in my hands.
S: Do you get a sense of what you're doing with these roots?
O: I'm collecting them to make a tea with them. It's to get rid of pain.
S: Tell me more.
O: My mother is in pain. She's about to leave this life and go back to where she came from.
S: Where does she come from?

O: Back where we all come from.

S: *Where is that?*

O: The sky.

S: *What happens next?*

O: (Sounding relieved) I make her the tea. We all tell her how much we love her, and she leaves.

S: *How do you feel about her leaving?*

O: I'm going to miss her, but we all know that we will see each other soon.

S: *How do you know this?*

O: It's something we all just know.

S: *Where do you live in this place?*

O: It's like a hut...well not a hut exactly because the outside is made up of stone with a thatched roof. I live in a village of sorts.

S: *What does your village look like?*

O: My village is mostly made out of stone, and we have stone streets. And there are some beautiful ornate designs on some of the houses, while some of them are bare or very barren like a wooden structure with thatched roofs, palm fronds roofs.

S: *Why were some made out of stone and some not?*

O: Some houses are older and as the populations grew, people would spread out and not have the time or the labor to create these big stone buildings and they would quickly create these new structures out of wood and thatch, which was fine because it could be hot there most of the time. Sometimes we receive storms that will blow in from the southeast most of the time, and sometimes it would rain and rain for days and days. We also have a system for flooding.

S: *What system do you have for flooding?*

O: We have canals that we dug, small canals around the roads that divert the water. We save a lot of the water that way too as it gets diverted into a reservoir that way.

S: *Are there modes of transportation there?*

O: We have carts with wheels on them and animals to pull these carts.

S: *What types of animals?*

O: It looks like a donkey, or something similar.

S: *Do you live there with anyone?*

O: My whole family lives there or around.

S: *Tell me about them.*

O: They're just loving people, everyone helps one another here (at this point she started sobbing). I miss my island.

S: *Tell me more.*

O: Everyone loves one another, there's no competition, and I feel so happy here, just so happy.

S: *What do you love the most about where you are?*

O: The people, my people.

S: *Tell me more.*

O: A big wave is coming (she started to cry again).

S: You can see this as an observer if you want to. What is happening?

O: It takes everything; everything is gone!

S: What happens to you?

O: We run and try to escape it. There's screaming, people trying to push each other up into trees or to hang onto something, but we're just no match for this wave.

S: What happens next?

O: I'm leaving the life behind now.

S: Tell me more about this. What do you notice?

O: I'm going back to where I came from (sigh of relief). I love it here.

S: Could you tell me about it? Where is here?

O: It's where everyone goes after they leave their physical life, a part of me is always here. I realize now that I'm always loved, always OK, there is no death. I'm always being helped.

S: Who is helping you?

O: It looks like me, just a smarter version of myself (laugh).

At this point I called in Olivia's Subconscious and started asking the questions that she had brought, as well as a few other health-related questions. These are a few that pertained to the past lifetime that she just left.

S: Subconscious, why did you show Olivia that life on that island?

O: We wanted to show her that that island was never really lost. While the actual island may be in pieces under the ocean, all her family is back again. She is back again. We want her to understand that she is always OK.

S: Where was this island?

O: It was an ancient place, some call it Lymuria.

S: Why does Olivia have a fear of the water?

O: It is from that lifetime where she drowned. It is important for her to understand that before that life she had wanted to experience drowning.

S: Why did she want to experience drowning?

O: Simply for her soul's expansion and experience.

S: Could you tell me why?

O: Basically, to fully understand how it feels to drown. As she overcomes this fear, it will be very powerful for everyone that knows her. They will see that they too can overcome their fears as well.

S: Does she understand this now?

O: Yes.

S: Now that she understands this, does she need to have a strong fear of water?

O: She can release this now. We're releasing it; it served its purpose.

S: What was its purpose?

O: The fear was a very strong motivator for her to look within herself.

S: Did she find out everything she needed to about this fear?

O: Yes, there is a clarity now, a realization that her dreams were actual memories from this time. She is also not alone. There are more people that have reincarnated from this time period sprinkled all throughout the Earth.

S: Why?

O: In order to learn and to remember what we once had within that beautiful and loving Lymurian civilization because the time is right for many to learn to have this again.

Olivia emailed me a week after her session to happily report that her fear of the water was completely gone. With this clarity Olivia divulged some wonderful, unexpected developments as a result of her session. She claimed her experience created a freedom within her allowing her to cast off the mundane repetition in her life, inspiring her to follow her true passions.

CHAPTER 9: THE DEATH OF THE QUEEN

Jen and I decided to work together whenever we could find the chance with both of our busy schedules. We had learned of her childhood and up until her adulthood when the visitors from Atlantis started showing up. Jen's tumor had shrunk dramatically and was no longer an issue, but the weight still hadn't come off. There was obviously something more that we hadn't uncovered yet. It was time to look into her mother's death. Since the lifetime that she experienced in Lymuria and Atlantis was traumatic in nature, I decided to take her to the time right after she left her body in that life so that she could gain more insight about that lifetime without having to re-live all the pain. This is her next session which took place in October of 2019:

S: Tell me more about your mother, the Queen.

J: Something horrible happened to her. I don't think we got her body back.

S: From your perspective and from where you are on the other side, can you see what happened to her?

J: We were set to bury her. She was killed by the visitors.

S: How was she killed?

J: The visitors had tricked her. They had been coming more and more to our island and one day they said that they demanded the crystals. And when my mother refused, they decapitated her in front of us with a laser like tool.

S: Were you there as well?

J: Our warriors grabbed me and pulled me out of there as soon as I saw it. I didn't see the aftermath of what happened afterwards to her body. It feels like we were all in a great big throne room. They cut her into pieces as they decapitated her in a seconds. They dismembered her and her parts just fell everywhere, and I felt her just rip away from us.

S: What do you notice about these visitors?

J: They looked very smug, very tall and blond, and very much like they are done playing games and are getting very nasty.

S: How are they dressed?

J: Today they have these metallic suits on that look a little like armor mixed with their basic metallic material that's made into jumpsuits. But this has extra stuff on it; it was their going into battle clothes. I think I noticed this from when they first walked in and it made me very nervous when I saw that. I thought, why did they have on this extra gear? They claimed to be peaceful, they claimed to be our ancestors, our cousins, and they were looking for our connection to our past, so why were they dressed like that?

S: They claimed to be your friends?

J: They somehow knew the legend of the two sisters, and they claimed it was destiny for us to work together.

S: Could you tell me more about your mother, about what type of a leader she was?

J: She was a perfect leader. I always felt that I could never be as good of a leader as she was. She was fair and just, and she was brave. She could fight, and fight, and win. She was very good. She had a long metal rod that she used that had a sharpened end on it, and that was her favorite weapon.

S: *Was she good with this weapon?*

J: Yes, she was trained in the steps of war.

S: *What are the steps of war?*

J: You can't lead an army unless you are trained in this. You have to become one of the best, and she was.

S: *What do you feel was one of the best things that she taught you?*

J: To be able to look at something terrifying and to be brave in its face. She taught me to hold my head up and to not respond to it, to never shrink to its overwhelming strength above you.

S: *Were you able to do this?*

J: I used this knowledge from my mother in my years of imprisonment, but I feel like I failed in the very brief time that I was the leader of my people.

S: *Why do you feel like you failed?*

J: There wasn't much time between her being killed, my inauguration, and then the death of our continent, maybe perhaps a few weeks at the most.

S: *Could you tell me more about your grandmother?*

J: She was more of a maternal mother than my mother was, but we were all taught and trained in the same way. She had more of a peaceful experience in her life though, so she wasn't as hardened by events that had occurred in her reign. It's important to know that the reign doesn't end with your death necessarily. You can decide for yourself if you would like for your reign to end and to be passed on.

S: *What do you mean by that?*

J: My grandmother passed it on to my mother so that she would be the ruler, even though my grandmother was still alive. But for me, it was different. I immediately became ruler with my mother's death.

S: *Were you ready to rule?*

J: No, but there is always an understanding that when there is an unexpected death, that is when your duty begins. There was a heavy sense of duty and sacrifice. I remember them both constantly reminding me of this. I wanted to do things that other kids were doing and playing, but I always had to be trained.

S: *Were you allowed to do those things?*

J: Not as much as other children. I was allowed to go and do certain things, but I had to be protected and prepared, and because of that it often created a sense of unhappiness towards my mother. My grandmother was very nurturing and very maternal. She was plumper, whereas my mother was more muscular. My grandmother would hug me and hold me and my mother was not as much inclined to do that.

S: *Do you feel as if you were ever in love with anyone?*

J: I believe I felt what I think is love for my young friend. Even though he had been taken away after that one day when we kissed, I met him again very awkwardly before my impregnation. He was presented along with several other well-decorated warriors, all of whose sperm was collected, mixed and inseminated into me during the ceremony. They were brought before us because they had earned many decorations of bravery and conquests, not because they were ruthless killers, but because they were recognized for using intelligence combined with maneuvering. I didn't recognize him at first but noticed the small scar on his forehead that gave him away.

S: *What did your young friend look like as a man?*

J: He had a very beautiful brown color to his skin. It was like a golden brown. It glowed and he had a very beautiful smile. His hair was always kept slicked very tightly back and it was kept in a braid.

S: *Tell me more.*

J: He made me laugh about how awkward this was going to be, and I enjoyed that. It felt like he wasn't afraid to speak to me. I felt that many people were afraid of me because they looked at us as different, not the same as them but slightly above them. But he didn't. Then, after the ceremony was done and I'd conceived my child, he would stop in to see me and the baby at the palace. He used to make jokes about how the baby looked like him.

S: *Did the baby look like him?*

J: It did.

S: *Did you get a sense if he was the father?*

J: I think we both hoped he was, but we knew there wasn't a real father in the child's life and there never would be. Had we been two different people, maybe we could've been together but I knew there was no way that I could ever leave my duty. It wasn't an option. I tried to push him away because I felt it wasn't be fair to him to live this type of a life, of being my friend and only my friend.

S: *Did he love you?*

J: Yes, I think he loved me very much and I did him, but there was no way we could be together.

CHAPTER 10: THE CORONATION

I was very excited to understand what the process was like for a Queen to be coronated in ancient society. I wondered what parallels there might possibly be to the current monarchy in our world and their traditions.

S: Could you tell me about your coronation process when you became the leader of Amun, Lymuria?

J: I see that I am in a very large room with a very large ceiling, and I'm on a square platform. I'm lifted above so others can see me. All around me there are so many people that line up all the way out of this room and throughout the many doors that open up. These people spread out all throughout the palace. This room that I'm in is not the palace, but a large holy place, a very special place people go for this type of ceremony, as well as for other special gatherings.

S: What do they do in this place?

J: It looks like right above me there is a large window with **the flower of life pattern** in it. It's a geometric pattern and when the sun shines through, it it's very bright. It has a lot of dimension to it when it hits the glass.

S: The glass or pattern does?

J: The refraction, the reflection of the light. The light that comes off of it is very lively.

S: Is there a purpose for this pattern on the window?

J: There is something that happens when you stare at it while you're meditating that helps you find the passage to the answers to your questions. It helps the brain think and grow and it enhances the communication when you try to communicate with the other realms.

S: By staring at this flower of life pattern or just this pattern in this window?

J: It seems like when you look at this pattern anywhere, it creates an imprint in the brain and almost like a key going into a lock, it unlocks it. If you begin to meditate in the right way, then it works in combination to open up a part of the mind that allows for ideas to come in and communication to be had. It seems like it's the same kind of route through which a lot of ideas that come to our people come. That is what this flower of life pattern is in this place. When you meditate while looking at this flower of life pattern, you haven't independently thought up something, rather it has been given to you through this route of transmission.

S: Do you know how the person is supposed to meditate while looking at this pattern?

J: It is a very simple type of meditation. You just need to relax and stare at it and the imprint of it in your brain will begin the process on its own. It's coded into you to do this.

S: Anything else that seems interesting or important about this?

J: The walls are a very light white and are a color that seems to have like an iridescence to it because of the way that the light from this window comes into the room. It's very white all around and there is a light shining down on to me and it is very hot. There is a lot of very heavy garb on my body; it feels very heavy with beads and details.

S: Tell me more about what you're wearing there?

J: There is a very heavy crown that I'm wearing made out of... it's not gold, but a heavier type of material. In the center of the crown there is a Red Crystal cut into a very large, red multifaceted gemstone. It's so heavy that it tips forward and I have to be careful to hold my head very far back with my nose up in the air, almost in order to keep it balanced, to keep it from falling. It hurts my neck a lot to carry it. It's something I definitely cannot drop because it would look like a bad omen for us, and it's been very bad already.

S: How do you feel about this coronation?

J: I feel good about this because I'm in a very vengeful mood, and I'm hungry to take action as a leader. I'm very eager to go and to do damage to those people for what they have done to my mother, but I know we have to do this first in order to legitimize our action against them.

S: Is there anything else you notice?

J: My daughter is there, and my grandmother is also there with me.

S: Tell me more about that.

J: I see them very clearly. They are wearing these white and grey silken robe outfits that are very long. They cover the whole body and go from the neck all the way down to the wrist and then down to the floor. And they both present me with two objects. The objects look like a globe on a pedestal, a golden sphere on a pedestal that has designs on it in gold as well. And then my grandmother presents me with what looks like a staff about two feet long. It's gold with ridges all along it like a Roman column.

S: Are there meanings to the things that were presented to you?

J: They're symbolic of what makes a good leader. The staff is about who has control, not about who has the biggest staff. That is why it is so small. And the globe is about who holds the world in their hands. You hold your people's world in your hands.

S: Are these things always given to the new leader?

J: Yes, my daughter hands me the sphere. I remember giving this to my mother at her coronation, and my grandmother gave my mother the staff. It must have hurt my grandmother a lot to have to hand this staff to me.

S: Could you tell me more about what else you see there?

J: My grandmother and daughter have their hair rolled back into a U- shape at the nape of their neck from behind their ears. It's rolled inwards and pinned back, and they both have their own crowns that they wear.

S: What about you? How are you wearing your hair?

J: Looks like it is in a top knot on the top of my head and then it is puffed out a bit and flattened down so that it's not sticking out above the crown, but exactly within the ring of it, like a pinned cushion that has been flattened.

S: Is there anything else that you do during this ceremony?

J: I remember there was a torrential downpour. At first it just looked like it might rain. There were these weird clouds in the sky that look like fingers had raked lines through them, like a giant hand had scratched their nails against the sky and made these indents. Then after the anointment was done by my grandmother, the skies just opened up and it filled with water quickly and everything just flooded for the next few days. For two days it floods and rains until it finally stops raining. The rain cancels the rest of the event, the rest of the coronation, the celebration part, but it doesn't really disappoint me because I don't think I was in the mood to celebrate at this point anyway. I was almost relieved that the rain took away the option to have any further ceremonies that night, that it cancelled the events.

S: *If it hadn't rained, what would you have done?*

J: When my mother became Queen, the celebrations went on for what looks like three days. There was a lot of dancing, singing, and different parades that look like they have floats almost. They make big animals out of what looks like paper and metal and they wheel them around using their bodies to propel them forward. Again, they have this type of firework that explodes and can make very beautiful star patterns without any color to them, but like a dazzling beautiful pattern. They do this for days, constantly at night. They would have these beautiful fire explosion shows.

S: *How did they make these?*

J: They had a type of gun powder that they mined, and they mixed that with some type of plant, and under a certain amount of heat it would get a spark.

S: *Did they have guns if they had gun powder?*

J: We don't have a large usage for guns, but we have the remnants of what looks like guns from our ancient ancestors that we were no longer able to use.

S: *Your ancient ancestors had guns?*

J: Yes, but in our culture the staff is more important. Some people have large metal pieces that they attach to the ends. Some attach knives and some attach balls with spikes on them. A lot of metal work was put on the ends of these staffs that could be metal, wooden, or mixed. They were very proud of their work with blades in our culture. We were more of a knife friendly culture than a gun friendly culture. This was because there was more civility using a weapon than using a gun. We understood guns as more of a tool than a weapon. We never used guns as a solution to our problems.

S: *Did your people understand certain moves of how to fight?*

J: We always had to be very spry, able to jump over this pole constantly, like a lot of jumping in a very swift way.

S: *Was there a specific fighting technique that you used?*

J: The technique was almost like a dance, and it was done in a way that was enjoyable for us. It was enjoyable so that we would ingrain it into our muscles, so we would not fear going into war. We would have it as part of our natural reflexes in a positive way because we were learning something with muscle movement while enjoying it. When you're enjoying something, it has a different effect then when you learn something and you're not enjoying yourself. Your body doesn't retain the moves, or become a natural reflex when you are in war if training is not done this way.

S: *Is this martial art form still practiced at all today?*

J: It is in some places, but now it's combined with other things, so there are elements of it that are still out there, but the original form of it is no longer practiced. There is still use of what's left of it in Japan, and definitely in the Polynesian Islands.

CHAPTER 11: THE WAVE THAT DESTROYED AMUN

With many clients recounting their own stories of the waves that flooded their beloved island, surprisingly the descriptions are uncannily the same. Danielle came to see me for a session because she felt stuck. She was sick of the mundane life she had and felt there was another calling for her that she had never quite tapped into. Danielle also wanted to understand a strange phobia of the water that she had felt her whole life. She felt compelled to see me and ask her Subconscious for answers. This is Danielle's session:

S: *What do you become aware of?*
D: The ground, it's lush, very green. There are flowers, many flowers. They are pink and green, white, and yellow.
S: *What do the flowers look like?*
D: They look very tropical. It's warm here, but not humid. There's a breeze and it smells very fresh and clean.
S: *What does this place look like? Could you tell me more about it?*
D: It's very green with many flowers and trees. There are hills, not really mountains but hills, big rolling hills.
S: *Where are these hills?*
D: Off in the distance, there's beach as well.
S: What does this beach look like?
D: The beach is beautiful; it is full of **smooth pebbles** and blue water.
S: *Is it rough or calm?*
D: It's very calm; it's like a beach bay. We're on an island, so there's water all around. The sand looks like small grey pebbles. It's not very sandy, but smooth so it doesn't hurt your feet.
S: *Look down at your body and see what your feet look like?*
D: They're women's feet, light brown.
S: *What about the bottom part of your body? What are you wearing on the bottom part?*
D: My legs are bare, but I'm wearing a small skirt. It's just a wrap.
S: *What does it feel like it's made out of?*
D: A beautiful light fabric. It's warm where we are.
S: *Does it have a color, this fabric?*
D: Hmm... it's bright yellow.
S: *What about the top part of your body?*
D: Just a small wrap top, it matches the bottom. My hair is brown and long and wild.
S: *What about your eyes?*
D: They're brown too, and my face is very fine with pretty features and a flatter type of nose. I seem to have some jewelry on, some rings and bracelets.
S: *What does it look like they're made out of?*
D: It looks like gold and leather.
S: *Where do you live in this place?*

D: I live in a house that's kind of round, like a hut but sturdier. It's not made of soft materials. It's made of stone and has a thatched roof. We all live together; I live there with my family.

S: *Tell me about them.*

D: I have a mate and a baby, a daughter. The rest of my family lives near me. All the huts are together, they're not spread out.

S: *What does your mate do during the day?*

D: He fishes, and he brings fish to the market.

S: *How do you feel about him?*

D: I love him.

S: *Tell me more about your baby.*

D: I love her; she's beautiful, she's little.

S: *Who lives in the huts near yours?*

D: Parents and grandparents, brothers and sisters. I can see them outside my window.

S: *You have a window? Tell me about it. What does the window look like it's made out of?*

D: It's just open, and it has a shutter made of the same materials as the roof.

S: *Do you have a bed in your hut?*

D: We do, we have nice furniture made of some type of tree wood. It's very comfortable. It's carved, beautiful and intricate.

S: *What do you enjoy doing there?*

D: Getting together with others. We laugh and we dance; the men go fishing and work. I work too; I help people. I'm kind of a doctor or shaman.

S: *Tell me more about that.*

D: I help women have their babies and help people when they're in pain.

S: *Tell me more about what you do when they are in pain?*

D: I do whatever they need; I have herbs.

S: *What type of herbs?*

D: We have many herbs that we grow and have access to. We can make a poultice. So, if someone is in pain or has a fever, I can give them a tincture or a tonic.

S: *How do you know how to do this? Were you taught by someone?*

D: I was trained by my mother, and her mother trained her.

S: *What is your favorite tincture that seems to be the most effective?*

D: Well you can use comfrey in things and that is very effective or oregano, there's so many to choose from. Our land has so many things available.

S: *How do you make these?*

D: I pick them, then I boil the roots of the herbs or the actual herbs, and then I heat them up. Once I heat them up, then I distill them down and then I have little jars that I keep them in.

S: *Say someone has a virus, what do you use for that?*

D: I would say oregano kills viruses, but our people don't get sick very often. Most of the things that we're treating are injuries or cuts. We're very healthy and we don't really have viruses or long-term illness.

S: *Do you get a sense as to why your people are so healthy?*

D: I feel as if we have some sort of immunity to things, but it could be perhaps because we do not experience that much stress here. There is plenty of food and water available for us and that makes us all more relaxed.

S: *What do you do when a woman is having a baby?*

D: We get them prepared. We coach them through their birthing process and make sure the head is down.

S: *How do you do that?*

D: We just know. There's a way to tell if the baby is head down or feet down and using your hand to see. You can put your hands on the belly and even spin the baby if it's in the wrong direction.

S: *What happens when someone dies on your island?*

D: We have a ceremony for them, and we put them on a raft that we make and put them out to sea.

S: *Do you prepare the body for the ceremony?*

D: We clean the body, then dress them, and anoint them with oils and perfumes as well as flowers. But we don't do anything that is invasive.

S: *How do people in your community view death?*

D: We believe that this time is just one time on Earth, and then you go to the spirit realm and you may come back. But we believe that you may come back as a different species like an eagle or bear. It doesn't always have to be human.

S: *What is the grief process like there?*

D: We don't grieve that much. We miss them, but we understand that part of life. If they have to leave, then it was their time.

S: *What type of ceremonies, if any, do you have there?*

D: We celebrate many things. We celebrate birth and we all support one another. It's very supportive and we're always with one another in our family tribe. Our family tribe is made up of all of our people, not just family. We love one another. There isn't any competition here. We help one another and take care of one another. We ensure the safety of everyone's babies, and we protect one another.

S: *How would you describe what most of the men are like there?*

D: They're gentle and loving.

S: *Is there anything else important or interesting about what you are looking at right now?*

D: No.

S: *OK, let's leave that scene and move ahead in time to where something important is happening. Be there now. What do you become aware of?*

Danielle started to breathe heavy and tears started flowing down her face.

D: There's a lot of water coming from the ocean. It's coming in fast; everything is going underwater!

Danielle started to become so upset that at this point I told Danielle that she could view this as an observer if she would like to.

S: *What does it look like?*

D: It looks like a massive wave that takes everything!

S: *What happens next?*

D: (Sobbing) I see my mate floating by face down in the water, I'm grabbing my baby and then the wave comes and we struggle to get our heads above the water, but I knew that I had to just relax and go with it. We die together. We all die. The island was just completely covered, the water just completely enveloped it. And it's just gone.

At this point Danielle took in a deep breath and almost looked as if a weight had been lifted from her shoulders.

S: *What do you notice now?*

D: I realize that we have drowned, but I still feel alive. It feels as if we just shed our bodies. Oh…(Danielle started to cry again)….my baby and mate are here. We're ok; everyone is ok.

S: *Tell me more. What is happening?*

D: We're just looking around, a little in shock; we feel alive but with no body. I'm sad but it feels different, like a heaviness. I just look around and I feel as if we're floating now.

S: *You're floating? Do you float together?*

D: Yes, we're floating away from that life. Looking down as I float up, I can see that this island was huge actually. It looks like it was in the South Pacific; now it's just under the water.

S: *Now that you have left that lifetime and can look at it from a different perspective, could you tell me what the purpose or lesson was that you were learning in that lifetime?*

D: The purpose of that life was to work as a healer, helping people. And being of service is an important part of my life. I realize that I saw that life because that is the work that I should do in this life. I also realize where my phobia of water came from because I feel it releasing from me! Almost like it has just been detached as it's no longer needed! Wow, this is incredible. (laugh) The phobia was just a catalyst for me to come here, for me to look inwards. In that way it was valuable; however, it is gone now.

I am always amazed at the wisdom that is given to the client during these sessions and the strategically placed lifetime that is shown to them. It is interesting how the past can affect the present, but only as a valuable trigger to allow the client to look inwards and move towards the healing and understanding that is needed. There are many people around the globe with these same unexplainable fears of drowning and of water that stems from this wave that once erased their treasured land. I later worked with Jen to recover her own memories of that fateful day when Amun saw its last moments above the water. Her memories detailed below may be very shocking and unsettling.

J: It was the first good day that we had in two days, and the sun came out that morning. There was a knock at my bedroom door, very early in the morning, earlier than I'm used to getting up. It was barely morning, the sun had not risen yet, and instead of the expected flooding at the beaches, I was told that the water had gone. I couldn't understand how the water could be gone since it had done nothing but rain for days. I quickly put on some clothes, grabbed my very long staff (the non-ceremonial one, my weapon) and I left my child with my grandmother. I took about five or six guards with me, ones that had been with me for many years, and they led me down to the beach. We got there just as the sun was coming up. It was dark at first so we couldn't see the full extent of the receding water.

69

There were many children and confused fishermen looking at their boats that had toppled over to one side. They were very upset and exasperated. They didn't know what they were going to do. The children of these fishermen were trying to run around and catch all the fish that were flopping on the dry land. The sun was coming up, and I could finally see the full extent of the water receding, and it was very creepy to look at. It was unsettling and didn't look natural, and everyone is reacting to it around me. Everyone is unsettled.

S: *What happened next?*

J: I see this kid point out to the water and he looked terrified. He had the most terrified look that I have ever seen on his face. I look over to see what he's pointing at and I see this wave coming towards us.

S: *What happens next?*

J: I know I'm climbing, I'm running, I climb up this wall and I get right up to the top of it. And right as I get up to the top, they (the visitors from Atlantis) scoop me up into that ball, that energy transfer device that takes me to them.

S: *Do you see the wave, or do you leave before it?*

J: I see everything; they make me see everything. I see that terrified child and what happened to him so clearly.

S: *From your perspective now, can you see what that child's full life was like?*

J: The child that I saw on the beach was about seven years old. He had a very simple life. I can see that he wore clothes that were made of loose linen, a grayish colored linen, and they were very loose on him. He was playing with his little brother who was about three, no more than three. They were both running around gathering the fish. And at seven and three years old they still would get up with their father every morning, and they would travel with him to the shore. And the seven year old boy would play with the little boy for a few hours on the shore in the shade every day. They would wait for their father to return with the day's catch, and when he returned, they would help. They would help separate the fish. The father would teach the children how to separate the fish into what was good and what was to be thrown back. Then they would help with pulling the nets. They were very strong for their age. They would pull these nets to town.

S: *Did they go to school there?*

J: Yes, they would also go to school. They always had options for children to learn writing, reading, and the basics of astronomy. These classes were done in the afternoon hours of the day into the evenings and the children would be sent home when the sun would set.

S: *Was it a school?*

J: There were small buildings that were made, they look like huts almost. There were a lot of open walls and thatched roofs so that it would stay cool for the children, but they would gather there, and they would meet with people who had been deemed educated enough that they could be teachers to these children. The teachers would be assigned and paid extra. They would be given food, grain, or would have a certain agreement with the fisherman or farmers. Sometimes, they would supplement their income with food and housing in exchange for doing this service.

S: *What did the language look like? Could you see?*

J: It looks like it has a lot of loops and flow to it, a lot of half C's with a dot in the middle, angles connected to these half C's and sharp ninety-degree angles connected to them. Also, there were lots of hooks connected to the letters. It looks very beautiful, very elegant and it looks very hard to read, but it's actually a very simple language. It doesn't take much for the young children to learn to read and write. It isn't very difficult. It is a very basic but profound language where one word could mean many things.

S: *So those boys that you saw, they help their father during the day, and they also help by pulling the nets into town?*

J: Yes, they have gathering places in the villages and the towns that populate our lands. And in these centers, they would bring their daily catch so people could come and purchase the fish that they would like for their lunch and dinner. Or instead of purchase they would trade. Trade was the most popular method.

S: *Do they have anyone who sells grains there or anything like it?*

J: They have linen bags filled with a grain, more like a small round granule, that is a tannish color and rough around the edges. It needs to be boiled for many hours with the water changed twice before you eat it.

S: *Where did these kids live? Did they live with their father and mother, or just their father?*

J: They have a father and mother, and three other sisters who spend their time with their mother assisting her with her chores and her needs for the household. Those children were all swept up by the wave.

S: *Tell me more about that?*

J: The look on this little boy's face when he sees the wave approaching is…it looks like he dies when he sees the wave, not when the wave hits him.

S: *Could you tell me more about that?*

J: The life got sucked from him as he stood there dead frozen in horror. The wave was so big, hundreds of feet tall… his little mind knew already that that was it…that his body was about to be demolished. The little one grabbed his brother's hand and it looks like he tries to pull him, and he just starts crying as the wave smashes into both of them and crushes them against the rock wall that was in front of us.

S: *What happened to them afterwards? What happened to their souls after they died?*

J: They wandered for a long time. They were very unsure of what had just happened and very confused and it looks like the young one is still… he is in a new body but is very stuck and very afraid of water. He feels very co-dependent on people because of this.

S: *What could help this soul?*

J: They are destined to read this book and when they do, it will resonate with them, and on a deep level they will understand and begin the process of healing.

S: *If there are many tragedies throughout history, are there many people that are stuck somewhere?*

J: There are many who are continuously stuck even when they unstick themselves, so it is a cyclical thing with humans.

S: *Why?*

J: I see it as a very integral part of evolution. Like a Yin to the Yang, it has to be. It has to happen in order for us to grow and develop from it.

S: *So, it's the instigator almost? The motivation to find out what's wrong?*

J: Yes. However, it's not sad on the other side. You're removed from human emotion over there.

S: *You were saying before that a lot of souls are trapped right now because of the destruction of Lymuria and Atlantis?*

J: Yes, many. And it seems that many, though, while that part of them is still trapped, they chose to be reborn at this time. Now is time for this information to return and act as a seed thrown into the mind that creates an understanding, healing, and a freedom for these people.

S: *How long ago was the fall of Lymuria?*

J: Twenty-five thousand years ago. **There are many similarities to what is going on now and what happened then, and the similarities are surfacing for a very specific reason. It is to break down that trauma and allow people to be free of this.**

S: *Is there anything else that is important about your experience during the flood?*

J: The water rose up, but the Atlanteans rose me up first. I was almost in a bubble that they had suspended. I couldn't get out of it; they wanted me to see everything. I watched this wave, this huge wave that just came out of nowhere. It was so big, and the water was just terrible. It was so powerful you could feel the energy of it, ready to just come crashing down and just smother everything and break it into a million pieces. And that's what happened when the first wave came down and just smashed, smashed everything. It smashed stones, wood, people and body parts. It just blew everything everywhere and just crumpled the whole coastline immediately. Then the water, it had to have been about fifteen feet deep, just kept quickly trickling in, and people got covered in water. You wouldn't see them anymore. The people were just trampling all over each other and taking babies and trying to hold them up in the air as if someone would just grab them, and then they would get sucked under as well. Or the babies would get pulled out of their arms, and you would just see them screaming and screaming. The screaming, you could just hear the screaming everywhere, it just didn't stop. Then there was a second wave that came from another direction and it met that other wave and it turned into this huge blob of death, just flowing over the land. When the two waves met, it looked like it created a bit of a whirlpool in the middle where it was just sucking people into circles, and they never came out.

S: *How did the island sink?*

J: The outer rim of the island was higher up then the center of the island, and when all the water came crashing in, it caused the island to sink.

S: *Is any of this island visible today or is it all under water?*

J: There are parts of the southeastern island that are still there above water, but you'll see just the rim of the island in certain places.

S: *Where?*

J: In the South Pacific on smaller islands, close to Thailand and the Philippines. Easter Island was once part of our land.

S: *Are there remnants of the island under water anywhere?*

J: Underwater, yes, there would still be a lot of the rock structures, but it would not be in order. It would be very weathered and tumbled and heaped. You would recognize it as something, but you really wouldn't be able to say what it was.

S: Were there any survivors on the outskirts?

J: There were some, a lot of them were warriors who were in the boats that were leaving or had been out looking at some of these other places where they had colonies being set up.

S: Where was that?

J: Places like Vietnam or China.

S: Where did the survivors go after the destruction?

J: There were people who left from the south side of the island and they sailed in the direction of what is now California. It took them about two months to get there safely.

S: What did they eat? Were they prepared at all?

J: No, and they barely had enough to eat. They were able to fish, but they had to ration the water very carefully, and they received some rainfall on the way over. It was deemed a miracle that they survived. They wouldn't have lasted that long normally so they felt that their survival was a miracle.

S: Why did they survive? Did something help them?

J: Part of their belief system was that they were chosen to survive, and that it was the guiding light of the Gods that brought them there.

S: What happened when they got there?

J: They found many natural entrances and cavern openings in the mountain there where they eventually made homes for themselves.

S: Why did they feel the need to go underground?

J: It was less underground, and more above ground then they had ever been when they lived on our continent. It was highly elevated there, so they didn't see it as an underground situation, but as a natural defense system that we had never had before.

S: Did they feel as if they were still in danger?

J: That became part of their DNA in many ways, that natural sense of distrust.

S: Are there any remnants of them still now?

J: You will find remnants of that civilization, but it won't be in the numbers that it once was. There are still people living there in that mountain.

S: Are there still people living there that are descendants from that island?

J: There are, but it is very difficult for the untrained eye to see them.

S: Why is that?

J: They're very good at maneuvering through their systems of caves and tunnels.

S: What do the people look like now that live there?

J: They have gotten whiter as a result of living underground, and they have also gotten slightly smaller, stouter and smarter.

S: Did their hair change color, or is it still the same?

J: No, it's still very similar to how it was. It tends to be very curly but every now and then there are still one or two children who are born with a streak of white or blond in their hair.

S: What do the people that still live in these mountainous caverns in California do there now?

J: They have their own set rules in that society and it's very basic. They spend a lot of time getting food.

S: What do they look like?

J: You would recognize them as being a human being. They would look different than you or I, but you wouldn't look at them and think they were aliens. You would just think they were from a different part of the world.

S: *How did they evolve?*

J: Over time they were able to bring back some of their culture, after the resettling and trauma was set aside. They tried to recreate with the same sense of compassion and bravery, what we had. Growing food became a big challenge.

S: *How did they grow food in a mountain?*

J: They created systems underground that grew mushrooms and diverted trickles of water through the inside of the mountain. That was how they received their fresh water and watered these things, but it's a heavy diet of things that could be grown in low light areas.

S: *Is there anything else about them that seems interesting or important?*

J: When they first explored the mountain, Mt. Shasta, they found within this mountain an open room of calm. This room of calm was put into place by one of the earliest sets of colonizers to this planet. These survivors, as well as the colonists before them, were able to step into this one area and it was very calming to anyone who stepped into it, almost like a dimensional plane where you could recharge. The survivors also found crystals inside there as well, and that brought back a lot of the traditions we had with our crystals. And by using them it kept those traditions strong.

S: *What kind of traditions did they do with the crystals?*

J: The traditions were mostly the ability to connect back with our ancestors, and these survivors kept transmissions within these crystals, and information was stored in them as well.

S: *Tell me more about that.*

J: Yes, they were able to gain a certain enlightenment using these crystals and communicating with the home planet. They were also able to touch these crystals and feel calm and steady, which helped tremendously at that time of so much uncertainty. When they went into this room, it became a circular room of peace. In it they could meditate, and they could bring themselves back to center.

S: *Can people do this now? Is that cave available to the public?*

J: It hasn't been seen; it's very hidden.

S: *Where is it hidden?*

J: Close to the top, but still deep inside. There is a little bit of light that comes in from above. There is a lot of that mountain that people don't get to see.

S: *Anything else interesting about this mountain?*

J: There's something green there, like an algae that glows. It comes from inside one of the caves. The room has a soft green glow.

S: *What was this green algae or the green glow used for?*

J: For lights, they were able to manipulate bioluminescence with crystals and water. It gives off a green glow. At first they used fire, but because of the exhaust they couldn't bring burning objects too far in. Once they discovered this strange algae that glowed, they started to use that instead even though some of the tunnels have openings that let some light through.

S: Why don't they come to the surface now that this is all over?
J: Is it all over? They have come to the surface, and they do not like what they see.

I, myself, had been to Mt. Shasta, California before this session with Jen. At the time I did not know to look for that beautiful room of calm, but I could feel the beautiful energy all over that mountain. It is amazing to think that there are still possibly descendants of those survivors living inside that mountain.

CHAPTER 12: EGYPT

In December of 2019, I took an exciting trip to Egypt to assist with teaching a QHHT class. From the moment I arrived, I could feel an immense power in this ancient land. As I am sure billions before me have been, I was drawn to the Sphynx and felt a unique energy pulling me towards it. During our class I underwent a regression with one of our participants. The first person who was picked at random to do the regression was a friendly young man named Jelmer.

I had already slipped into hypnosis and had no idea that anything strange was happening at the time, but around me powerful energies of the universe were at work. Before Jelmer could speak and lead me further, an unseeable force gently pushed him to the ground and kept him on the ground till our session had ended. Another practitioner named Marco stepped up and had to take over. One of the practitioners in the class filmed the whole thing. Whenever I have had doubts about writing this book, I would remember this session and that force that was obviously guiding us.

Jelmer: What do you see around you?

S: I see jungle, a lot of jungle, and woods. It's really hot and buggy. There's a lot of hot standing water around. I feel so hot. There are lots of big cats in the distance because I just heard one and it had a guttural sound, the sound goes right through me. I have a spear (At this point unbeknownst to me, Jelmer had started to hang his head before he then fell down to the ground. He told me later that he had never had an experience like that before. He could feel some sort of loving presence lightly pushing him to the ground. He was only able to get up after this session was over. Marco, another practitioner, sat up out of his chair and quickly took over in Jelmer's place.)

Marco: What do you see?

S: Lots of jungle, a big canopy of trees. I'm hunting. I just have this overwhelming sense of deep unworthiness; I'm hunting, and my trap didn't catch any fish.

M: So, there is water?

S: Yes, it's just moving water. I just feel sad; I just have this deep sense of sadness. Nothing I can do is good enough. I feel like I'm not worth anything to the people around me.

M: There are people around you?

S: In the village there are.

M: Go where you live.

S: I live with my father. We live in a really rudimentary place. There are like sticks and animal skin for our house. I feel as if my father really hates me, he hates me.

M: Do you know why?

S: No.

M: Are you young or old?

S: I'm young. Oh I know why he hates me because my mother died when she gave birth to me, and whenever he sees me it reminds him of this.

M: Are you male or female?

S: *My body is rather frail, but I'm a young boy, almost a man.*

M: Are you wearing anything on your feet?

S: *No, I have lots of skins on my body.*

M: What color?

S: *Light colors with spots on it. Looks like the animal was tan and had white spots.*

M: Do you see your hair?

S: *It's long... I feel very sad, like no one likes me or wants to be mated to me because I don't have any skills. I just heard my name. It feels like there is something happening right now. There are some messengers that just showed up. They say they have been sent by the women rulers to find information about a different land and civilization near us, and they need a group of people to explore this land and report back what they found.*

M: Do you want to go?

S: *No, I don't want to do that because people don't always come back when they are sent out to do things like this.*

M: So, what do you do?

S: *I don't know why they chose me because I'm kind of young for this, but I have a feeling that my father asked if I could go so he could get rid of me.*

M: Because he hates you?

S: *Yes, he hates me.*

M: What happens next?

S: *I have to get ready and pack my stuff. I have some grains that I'm going to take. I have them wrapped in skin and I have some dried meats and fruits, and the woman who make the medicines are giving me some stuff to take.*

M: Do you know the other people who are going with you?

S: *No, I don't know them, but there are two others who are chosen to come with me.*

M: What are they like?

S: *They're both older than me. One is a shorter man and has curly hair. He has an animal with him that looks like a type of camel that I don't recognize and another man who seems a lot taller than the both of us.*

M: How do you feel about these people?

S: *I don't think I like the taller one very much because he's grumpy, but I really like the shorter one because right away the shorter one starts telling us stories. They are mainly about his life, but it makes me feel comfortable. Normally someone as young as I am does not go on this type of a journey.*

M: And you don't want to go?

S: *No, but I really don't care if I come back. I don't want to be anywhere.*

M: Let's move forward to an important day. What do you become aware of?

S: I hear screams from the shorter man. His animal was eaten while we slept. He loved that animal so much; it looks like one of the big cats got it and ate it. It had all of our food on it though, so I don't know what will happen to us. All of our food and the skins that we brought with us are gone. Now the taller man and shorter man are arguing. The taller one wants to go back. He says that we need to go back because the further we go the further into our pit we go. The shorter one says that there is no food to go back to, so we should keep going.

M: Do you see where you are now?

S: *On a reddish dirt skinny path in the jungle traveling West is about all I know.*

M: Do you know where you are going?

S: *We only know to go West, that is where these other people live.*

M: OK, let's leave that scene and move to another important day. Tell me what is happening.

S: *It's overwhelming, I don't know how to describe it, it's a huge sculpture. I have never seen anything like this before. It's a large sculpture of a jungle cat. The cat's eyes are so intricate and beautiful that it's overwhelming. We have never seen anything like this before. None of our people know of anything like this.*

M: Can you touch it?

S: *Yes, it's so big. We are in shock as to how people could have made this. The sculpture is so breathtaking that we make a fire by the paws of this large sculpture and we just set up camp there.*

M: Move around this sculpture and see what you see, is there anything else around?

S: *Yes, there is moss growing on it, and vines, and going up it there are blocks holding up the face, these sand-colored blocks holding up this lion- like cat face made out of what looks like sandstone.*

M: Can you walk around?

S: *Yes, it looks like water has come up to it. Running water is nearby, close. I can hear it, and it almost feels as if you can feel the energy of this sculpture.*

M: You can feel this energy?

S: *Yes. We do not want to leave. It's like when you see something so amazing that you can't take your eyes off of it. We stay there until we fall asleep, but we don't sleep.*

M: You don't? What happens?

S: *As I drift off to sleep, I instantly feel something strange. I feel as if something scans me and the back of my mind to see if it's OK for me to go in.*

M: In the sculpture or where?

S: *I don't know. I feel half awake and half asleep. It feels as if something scans me and then starts pulling me. I'm not conscious enough to know exactly what is happening, but now I feel like I'm going down really deep into it, this sculpture, miles down.*

M: How do you feel?

S: *I feel that feeling you feel when you are half asleep. I feel calm, almost sedated, but after going down underneath this sculpture, I'm taken to another area where there are records and I feel as if I'm being scanned again.*

M: How does it feel when they scan you?

S: *Very strange because I don't really see anyone doing this to me, it feels like whoever is doing this is lighting up the back of my brain. It seems they use the back of my brain to show me the records. Now I'm looking into myself from a different third perspective, almost as if I'm seeing into myself, this is weird.*

M: What do you see?

S: *I see my life and I see all my problems. I created these problems so I'm fixing them now, here and now. I feel like it's fast, whatever, whoever this energy is, it is helping me fix my problems and the parts of my life that have been a problem, and now it's complete. Now whoever they are that is doing this to me are showing me our mother island and the wave. We need to get back to tell the others. The island of Amun has just gone into the ocean. Survivors are coming. We need to get back.*

M: Is there anything you can do?

S: *No, I'm supposed to tell my people back home. We do not live on the island that just went under water. We live on the outskirts. I need to get back to help the survivors who will be seeking shelter with us.*

M: What happened next?

S: *I wake up, I look at the other two people with me, and I can tell by their faces that they had similar experiences.*

M: What happens next?

S: *We all understand what we need to do. We need to turn back.*

M: What happened when you went down beneath the face of the sculpture?

S: *I feel I have completely changed, and I can tell that the other two have changed as well.*

M: Do you feel this knowledge changed your body?

S: *My body still looks the same, but I feel completely different, almost whole. The shorter one keeps talking about how we went into the dream. He keeps going over it and wondering if we could figure out a way to do this again, to bring this method of fixing one's problems back to the village. We all feel the difference in ourselves after this experience; we know we have been changed.*

M: How do you feel?

S: *I feel that I want to go back to the village to live my best life. I feel completely changed for the better; I feel complete.*

M: What happens next?

S: *When we get back, we share our stories of the stone sculpture and the visions of our homeland Amun and the flood that sank it. Survivors started arriving shortly after as we had expected.*

M: Let's move to the last day of that life. What do you become aware of?

S: *I'm old and surrounded by my loved ones. I had children. My mate is crying and thanks me for our life. I'm just leaving my body.*

M: What do you notice on the other side?

S: *I meet up with my other two journeymen on the other side of that lifetime, and we talk about when we will meet again. We agree that it will be thousands and thousands of years later. These stories will be hidden until then because people will not understand the enormity or the power of this information until a certain time. I see that the time is now for these stories to be remembered and retold as we enter into the Great Awakening. It seems the part of our brains that we need in order to process this information has been awakened. Humanity only advances in cycles, not on a straight and linear path. This was the plan all along. I see and understand now that the sculpture that we saw was the Sphinx, although the face has changed over the years. When we were there in that lifetime, it was not surrounded by pyramids, but I can tell that it was the marker into the entrance of what you call Atlantis. Our civilization and our homeland were on the outskirts of what you would call Lymuria, although we called it Amun, our home.*

My regression in Egypt was so powerful to me that I wanted to find out more. Not only did I want confirmation, but I wanted to figure out how it was related. Jen agreed to work with me under hypnosis to see if she saw anything more about this lifetime in Egypt. After I put her into a deep state of hypnosis, I found she was able to easily locate and view my lifetime there.

S: Let's drift and float over the lifetime I had when I went to the Sphynx thousands of years ago. Can you see that lifetime?
J: I found it. I see you.
S: What do you see me doing there?
J: You are at the Sphynx. I see you downloading some information during a dream.
S: Can you describe what happens to me?
J: It looks like an ultraviolet light that comes out of the Sphynx and into you, that's the best way to explain how you came into contact with that energy that is in there. It's not a physical download but like a download of information that opens up something in your brain, yours and the two other people with you there. You all seem almost in awe as you travel back. You know that you have to go back; there's nothing left there for you at the moment except this overwhelming need to go back and to find these survivors who you know you're going to meet. As soon as the three of you return, they start to show up. There are just a few of them at first that show up but more and more over time.
S: Who exactly are these people?
J: These are the people who escaped the cataclysm in Lymuria. You live in a village off the island, one of our colonies. My mother was the one who, before her death, sent the messengers out to your outpost to find out more about the Atlanteans. When the three of you were at the Sphynx, you all were shown the cataclysm in your dreams and were told to go back to help the survivors.
S: Tell me about the survivors?
J: It seems like at first the survivors try to use the resources that they have that are left in the little areas that they are stranded on. Then they begin to journey outwards, and those who are lucky to survive the journey tend to find your settlement, your camp. Your camp is very different because of the three of you. Once the three of you come back there is an enlightened sage aspect to you now. Because of your experience within the Sphynx, you see things differently, so you're able to guide that society a bit more, and you're more advanced in that way, not in technology, but in a different way of treatment. Your societal rules are enhanced by this. The people you helped were helped by this as well and they became better as a result. But your camp got too big. There were too many people who came to you, and you ran out of resources. The water supply was not enough for everyone and it

looked like the climate was changing around you, as well, very rapidly.

S: *Why?*

J: The cataclysm with the wave caused some climate change issues. It looks like it made things very dark. The sky was affected and was dark for a while.

S: *Tell me more about the sky after the cataclysm.*

J: It looks very ashy and sooty for quite some time, and it affects a lot of eco-systems too which is why you all begin to run out of food as well. The things you had known to do to keep your people alive can no longer be depended on. So, from there your journey begins. You take people back to the area of the Sphynx, and you begin a new colony there. There were just a few at first, but I see you make this journey several times. You bring many people back here. Because you are the younger one of the three, you are able to continuously do this longer. They don't entirely abandon the community where you first spend your life, but it continuously seems to stay an outpost for the Egyptian empire.

S: *What is better about the area where the Sphynx is located?*

J: The inundation of the river Nile there allows for a dependable growth of food. And it is very lush and jungle-like at this point. It looks very different from the way it does now.

S: *Were the Pyramids there at that time as well?*

J: No, not at that point. Those will come after this, a few thousands of years later. The Pyramids are definitely a product of the technology that stemmed from the originators bringing that technology from the home planet.

S: *So, I bring people back to the Sphynx to set up a new colony and that is the beginning of the outpost of Egypt?*

J: Yes.

S: *What happens to that colony that I brought there?*

J: It begins the primary culture of ancient Egypt, the very beginnings, what we know of as ancient Egypt.

S: *So, the people that I brought over at first were Lymurians?*

J: Yes, they were the refugees. Some were also the people of your community who chose to go to this new outpost for a different life. A lot of younger people wanted to go to start families and live there. There is some type of religious cult that was set up there after your death, because it seems you wrote a book.

S: *Could you tell me more about that?*

J: The book you wrote begins a lot of the folklore that we understand now about ancient Egypt. You wrote a book about the stories you heard while you were transporting people back and forth. You decided that there needed to be something that commemorated the people and the stories that you heard of those who died, so that the understanding of what happened in that land and to those people would not be forgotten in time. I see that you are doing this again in this life.

S: *Tell me more.*

J: It looks like the first version was written in the very basic Lymurian language. It was a very easy language to learn to read and write. Later, the book was revised and had a much more ornate cover made out of gold and metals. There were even different types of metal brackets on it. That wasn't made by you, but that was a later version with hieroglyphic type writing in it. And it was an adapted version of your work, so it wasn't the exact translation, but their translation of what you had written. Some things were changed slightly to fit their needs.

S: Did any of it end up in a published book that is around now?

J: Yes, the basis of it is still there. The name of that book is **The Egyptian Book of the Dead.** Even to this day if you read that book and you read between the lines, there is more to what is being said there. If you read it looking at it from that view point you will see how it could have been misinterpreted over the years as to what it really was. These were the stories that you collected about the people and survivors of my island.

S: How did they find the writings that I wrote?

J: It looks like writings were kept in a religious sacred community. They were kept very carefully. It looks like there was even a stone altar underneath it. They kept it in a small cave, a little boxed area that was meant for it.

S: Anything else you see about it that looks important or interesting?

J: It looks like it has a very large role in the development of the Egyptian religions because of the importance to the people who first developed that community. Even though its true meaning was lost, it still is very powerful, even misinterpreted.

S: What would you say the true meaning of this book was if you could summarize it?

J: Commemoration of the people that were lost in that sacrifice is what comes across as the meaning. This is essentially what you are doing with the book you are writing now. You're back again to do this again, so that the memories are not lost. You have planned this. That is important for you to understand now.

This session with Jen helped me to understand why I have such a strong desire to share this knowledge. I was shocked but found a deep comfort in knowing that I had written this book before.

CHAPTER 13: A PRISONER IN ATLANTIS

I have had other clients recount their experiences of being an experimental subject to the Atlantean scientists, but no one who was an actual prisoner like Kala. I was interested to find out more about what this was like, and if any good came from these experiments.

S: *Now let's move to after the visitors from Atlantis have captured you, and have taken you to their continent. What do you become aware of? You can view this as an observer if you would like to.*

J: As I was a prisoner in Atlantis, the Atlanteans were always trying to find that immunity that I had. They were always doing blood work and things with electricity on me. They would study my brain and heart and how the connection works with my body and these red crystals. They would study and study and still couldn't figure out how the immunity was created for our people. That had always been the focus of what they were looking for.

S: *What else did they do to you?*

J: They found many different ways to torture me, to see if I would break. I was treated like a lab rat, an animal. They were also using me constantly for their invasive, cold experiments.

S: *Did they ever test that virus on you to see if you would get it?*

J: They left on many occasions open opportunities for me to receive this virus, and it had very little effect on me.

S: *Tell me about that.*

J: There had been very little effect on me because my blood type carried something that worked against it. My people had used the red crystals to protect our people with immunity, so they did not contract illnesses on our island. We had our share of pain, but we didn't have colds or viruses that came from people, only from animals that may get illnesses. There was a lot of work that was done to make sure that our meat was prepared well for this reason. Our animals were kept in certain types of quarters. There were many similarities with the Hasidic Jewish culture in that meat had to be kept in a certain way. This was because we were protected, but the animals weren't. That was a way that you could end up causing illness to yourself, was from an animal. We normally ate a very natural plant-based diet. **Eating a plant-based diet** is one of the strongest activators of memories for some people, because that diet activates the specifics of that previous existence.

S: *What are the benefits of activating this existence?*

J: To help pull together for many people little mysteries of their life that they've never fully understood, until they put all the pieces together like we are and understand a different version of their history.

S: *Did they do or say anything else to you when you were a prisoner there?*

J: The first set of torture they used on me was that they would force me to re-watch the flood and the wave over and over and over again. They would play the sounds of the screaming all day long while I was awake and while I was asleep. They tried to wear me down so that I would show them how to communicate. I would not do it. My mother made me swear that I would never ever show them; my grandmother made me swear this as well. They also would put me in this gorge, and they would put other people in there with me, children, men, innocent people. Then suddenly I would hear them yell out, and this water would just come crashing in. Then I would be lifted up above it all to watch these people drown. They were their own people, usually people from the third ring, children of slaves, the working class that they had no need for anymore. And they would make me watch that over and over again. This water would just come flowing through and drown everyone around me, and I would have to watch as their bodies floated to the top. Then they would isolate me for long periods of time.

S: *How long would they isolate you for?*

J: Months, with darkness and isolation, and no one to speak to. But, they soon realized that that wasn't going to be as effective with me.

S: *Why wasn't it?*

J: Because in the darkness I was able to meditate in a way that I was able to speed up time for myself.

S: *How did you do this, and how fast did you speed it up?*

J: I sped it up fast enough so that it was almost as if I didn't feel it. It was almost like they were doing me a favor by doing this type of torture because I was able to block out all my senses and still communicate with the others.

S: *Who would you communicate with?*

J: Whoever was on the other side at that time.

S: *And who was that?*

J: The beings of energy that were left on our home planet. They didn't have bodies necessarily, but they could still communicate. You could still feel what they were trying to say.

S: *What did they say to you?*

J: To be patient, over and over again.

S: *Tell me more about how you speed up time?*

J: I was able to speed up time within myself. I was less aware of time, so I was able to manipulate it as a distraction. It was something very unique to having my senses dulled and being deprived of light and fresh air and human touch. After a certain amount of time those are the things that make time relevant and without them you could zip through it. And when I would emerge from these periods of confinement unshaken, it would infuriate them. They would shave my head so it would not need to be cared for. It's funny, I recognize some of these captors now in my current life.

S: *Tell me about that, who are they now?*

J: Some I have worked for here on this island; some of them I have met in London, Egypt, many places. I'm just realizing this now, but in Atlantis the captors changed over the years.

S: *Why?*

J: I outlived many of them. It became harder and harder for them to keep track of me, and I used that to my advantage.

S: *They had to keep track of you?*

J: They had to keep track of what type of torture they were doing to me and what type of punishments I should receive and what kind of lifestyle I should be given.

S: *What kind of lifestyle did you have?*

J: I had very uncomfortable jail cells, several different cells that would be equivalent to a maximum-security cell or jail of our time now for many years, for the first forty to fifty years that I was there. But then when I became old, they didn't see me as a threat. They saw me as an old-women and instead of executing me, they gave me a very small apartment. The apartment also had high security, but it was more comfortable. I had a bed, a kitchen, a table and a comfortable seat. I also had a window. I hadn't had a window for years and I also had a bathroom.

S: *What was the bathroom like?*

J: It was more of a hole in the floor, but they had a system of plumbing that involved bringing in fresh water and getting rid of old water. We did not have something that advanced where I was from.

S: *From where you are right now, can you tell whether or not you had a pre-birth agreement with these captors?*

J: It was more than an agreement. This was a necessary developmental point in our planet's evolution, and I was put there because of my previous experiences. I agreed to this even though I had hesitancy right before. There was a feeling of "does this really need to happen?"

S: You had hesitancy about this life before you lived it?

J: I did, but I knew that it did need to happen.

S: *Why did it need to happen?*

J: **There were many different things that occurred as a result of this life that have led us to where we are now. And where we are right now is exactly where we are supposed to be. If things had not catapulted us to this moment, we wouldn't be as evolved as we are. We are ready for what's about to unfold in our next evolutionary phase.**

S: *What is about to unfold?*

J: **There is more of an enlightenment coming, a period of time where people will shed their masks and embrace who they are, a time of understanding, a golden age in many ways.**

S: *When is this supposed to happen?*

J: It has already started, and it has been happening, but it's a process that is very detailed through cause and effect. It has been happening for thousands and thousands of years.

S: *So, we're entering into a golden age?*

J: A golden age of remembrance in many ways. It's coming full circle into a golden age of what we originally had. Without the destruction of these civilizations there was no way for us to evolve and to get passed it, because we already saw what these Atlanteans accomplished with their technology and realized that they needed to be removed because they were not embodying all that we needed.

S: *What do you need?*

J: There has to be a mix of compassion and understanding along with the scientific and technological advancements. The two civilizations needed to come together to help one another and continue to create, but if that was not going to happen, then it needed to be destroyed and spread out so that it would come together thousands of years later to create the next phase of human beings.

S: What is the next phase of human beings?

J: It is a better person who embodies the right characteristics and is not held back by the wrong characteristics. It is a more perfect human being. But not perfect in the picture-perfect sense, just a more mentally aware individual. We are moving forward into a world where people are not subjugated by their bodies and are not counted as cattle, not corralled by people's ill intentions. There is a breaking away of this; it is the beginning phase of a freedom for people.

S: I have heard that many of the people that are walking the planet today are the same people that died in the cataclysms. Why is that?

J: There are many, many of them. Some have chosen to complete themselves and have finished their journeys and have possibly moved on to other dimensions, but there are many, many who are still working this out or plan to work this out in this lifetime.

S: What are they working out?

J: **There is a great trauma that comes along with such terrible events and for those who refuse to learn the lessons, they are doomed over and over again to repeat it**. That's why you see throughout history and religion so many cleansing floods or plagues. It's a chance for them to learn again what they have failed to learn from the last one.

S: What were they supposed to learn?

J: Many wanted the chance to rebuild their lives; many people who were killed in the initial flood craved that which they had lost. And they wanted the chance to regain what they had lost. If you do not regain what you have asked for, you will continue to do this over and over again until you do.

S: So, rebuilding your life and getting what you want is important?

J: Yes, what you want is also seeking you.

I then asked to speak with Jen's Subconscious to ask some personal questions for Jen, and these are some of the answers the Subconscious gave that I am at liberty to share:

S: Why does Jen keep having the wave dream?

J: It was just part of the torture. She can see this now. It felt advanced but old at the same time.

S: You have said before that Jen is to write about this and share this story. Is there anything else about that that you would like to tell Jen?

J: She needs to understand that there are **millions of people who will relate to this story**. There are millions of people who will actually recognize themselves in this story and it will begin to open their minds.

S: Will Jen's book be successful when it is completed?

J: Yes, but there will be something very, very liberating about this story finally being told after so many thousands of years. It will not affect her next life once she gets this story out.

S: Any advice you would like to give her to help her write?

J: Remember that this is the liberation from the past; the story will free you!

CHAPTER 14: INSIDE ATLANTIS

Many have talked about the energy that the Atlanteans had tapped into as well as been curious about this highly advanced society. This is another one of Jen's recounts, while under hypnosis, of her stay as a prisoner in Atlantis.

S: *Could you tell me more about this energy that Atlantis had?*
J: They had harnessed a specific type of energy that they had obtained from the people who came before them, from their home planet.
S: *Do you get a sense of where that home planet is?*
J: From beyond our earthly galaxy, in the stars, behind the Big Dipper. The Atlanteans wanted me to tell them how to use the red crystals and no matter what form of torture they used on me; I would not tell them. They could never get this technology. The power was too great and in the wrong hands it would destroy too much. I understood why the ancestors didn't want them to have it.
S: *Is there anything else about the red crystals that seem important?*
J: The importance of these crystals was the ability to communicate back with our ancient ancestors and our ancient home. They could not do it even though they had remained technically advanced from their time of arrival and had even grown technically. We were able to use these crystals even though we had lost a lot of that technology. We had the most important thing that we were supposed to come with, which was compassion, and they were void of compassion.
S: *They were void of compassion?*
J: Yes, they were a very strict and stern group of people, perhaps not all of them, but the ones I came into contact with were all the same, very opinionated and demeaning.
S: *Were they like this to one another or just to you?*
J: Especially me, but they had a specific class system in their society. People were not allowed to rise and fall in their class. You were born into a certain class and treated that way with no ability to maneuver.
S: *What were the classes of Atlanteans like?*
J: The wealthiest were educated highly and were kept within the inner ring of the city. The inner ring of the city was where all of the buildings were more advanced. There were many areas of discovery, and the schools were highly advanced. The second ring were people who were more of an upper middle class, but they kept to themselves and would often try to integrate with the upper echelons, what they considered the more important people, but they understood they would never be fully accepted. The most you could hope for would be to possibly marry someone from the inner ring, but even then, your children would still be considered middle class. Then the work force which also included slaves lived in the third outer most ring.
S: *Who were the slaves?*
J: The wealthy would have people that they would keep as slaves if they felt that the person owed money or products to someone. They would have them enslaved for a certain amount of time until they worked their debt off, which is how I received my helper.

S: Tell me more about your helper?

J: She had been enslaved at a younger age as part of a debt her father and mother owed to a first-class family, and so she was given the job of taking care of me.

S: Could you tell me more about the people of Atlantis? Did they have any leaders of churches or priests there?

J: Not that I'm aware of and not that I saw when I was there. They were more a church of science than that of belief. They operated as a school of thought. The most respected people were the most educated who came up with the more technological advances. Those were the people you would go to and seek out and listen to them talk, but you wouldn't particularly go to a building once a week to discuss faith and beliefs.

S: What did they believe in? Were they spiritual at all?

J: They were very interested in scientific advancement and in harnessing technologies and developing them.

S: Were they aware of reincarnation or any similar belief?

J: I don't believe they felt a strong connection to that, or it had been shut off in their minds. They had evolved past that and did not feel the need to lower themselves to something they could not concretely see and feel and know. It made them a colder being because of this.

S: What happened when a person died in that society?

J: The people were reduced down to ashes, or crystals and given to the families. There were no cemeteries or burials at sea because they understood how it would contaminate the waters that surrounded them.

S: How did they shrink their loved ones down?

J: They would burn them using a type of synthesizer that would turn them into a token of sorts that would be given to the family.

S: Would the family grieve?

J: Yes, they would. However, they were more detached when it came to death. They accepted it as a rite of passage, a next step. It wasn't as emotional as we would have had it on our island. We would wrap our dead and bury them. We had periods of time afterwards for the family to console one another.

S: Tell me more.

J: We would wrap them in a gauze-linen like material, not white, but a creamy brownish color. We would clean them and anoint them with flowers and oils.

S: What type of oils?

J: They would come from the sap of a tree and distilled down into an oil. It has a very fresh piney scent to it. It would help keep the body smelling fresh as it was prepared.

S: Where would the body be put after it is prepared?

J: Many people would have plots for their families on their properties and that is where they would go. My family would be buried within a family tomb underneath our palace.

S: Were there many people buried there?

J: Yes, many. I remember carving into the walls and seeing who was there and it would also give you information about that ruler, of who they were, what they were famous for, and what they accomplished. There were so many of them it would go on and on because the walls were all a dark grey stone.

S: Tell me more about your time in Atlantis. Is there anything else they would do to you after they captured you?

J: For the first few years they did many, many experiments on me.

S: What other experiments did they do?

J: They tried many different ways to figure out how I was able to utilize that red crystal. One experiment that they did was something that felt like flashes of light, blue and purple light being flashed at me.

S: They would have lights flashing on you?

J: That was just one type of experiment where I would start out by being strapped to a table but in a standing position. My arms and legs would be strapped and they would even put something around my mouth. Then they would flash the ultraviolet light at me. It doesn't necessarily hurt but it hurts my eyes a lot and it makes me feel a little crazy because it goes on and on for hours.

S: What do you do during this time that they do this to you?

J: I try to go into my head and think of ways to escape. I think of what's different from the night before; I try to notice the patterns they have, any escape routes I may see. I try to keep myself sane by doing that and I try as much as I can to not meditate. I think they will figure out more about how this energy is channeled if I do. I try to keep myself thinking constantly about my escape, even though I know now that I never will.

S: **How is the energy actually channeled?**

J: It's something that takes a very long time to cultivate and is taught at a very young age, but it is a set of movements that allow you to open up and receive it. The channeling must be done by someone who is a receiver. It can't specifically be done by just anyone.

S: How does the person know if they are a receiver for this energy?

J: They can feel it; they feel it and they know. But it needs to be taught, it is not something that is just an instinct. It looks almost like a prayer in the movements and then an incredible focusing must be done where you feel yourself focusing from the middle of your brain, from behind the eyes. Right in there, in that area. There is a gland there, and it must be focused and then the stone must be raised up and put toward your heart and absorbed into you.

S: So, it's just the red crystals that are used for this purpose?

J: Yes.

S: What does the prayer do? Could you tell me more?

J: The prayer clears you up and opens up the space.

S: What is the prayer?

J: It's not specifically a prayer, but its movement that opens you up by allowing yourself to clear out all your energy to become a receiver.

S: Tell me more.

J: The movement looks like when you first go into a shower and you allow the hot water to go down just to the back of your head down your spine and relaxing it and bowing down toward it, with your hands up by your eyes. Then your hands go down to your knees, then you come back up. It's a movement that's done in repetition. You use that repetition to put yourself in a trance and then you are ready to focus. Once you are there you can feel a jolt in your body, like a snap in electricity, and you know you are ready to start focusing. Then you stay very still and breathe very deeply, and you go inwards into the brain as you raise up the gem and bring it to your chest and allow it to be absorbed into you. And then you just go through a worm hole. You can then travel through it mentally to communicate with the home planet.

S: *What do you do when you communicate with your home planet?*

J: There's really not much there, just energy vats that are left of people. They can't communicate in words with you, but they can communicate in feeling and give you answers to things that you are figuring out at the moment.

S: *What will that feel like?*

J: It feels like good or bad feelings that they will transmit to you. You get your answers through the way they feel, not by words. They seem speechless, there are no need for words at this point, almost like they're not ghosts, but a vapor-like energy.

S: *Can you communicate with them right now?*

J: Yes.

S: *What happened to them?*

J: They had a very long history as an experimental planet, and they ran out of resources. They had neighbors on other planets who helped to deplete their resources as well and they fought each other till there was very little left. Then there was a time of transition for that planet and they sent people out to seed throughout the universe and those that were left evolved into these big beings, this spirit like energy because they hit a point in their evolution that allowed them to transition into this. And these are the only beings that are on their planet now. But it was a process of removing the arguing, the resources, the fighting, and breaking it all down into having no reason to do any of those things that allowed them to transition, so it was a very long arduous process of them remembering the goal, which was to morph into this.

S: *So, you don't meditate or talk with your home planet so that the captors don't figure out what you are doing?*

J: Yes, I only did when I was in solitude.

S: *So, you meditate while you are alone?*

J: Yes, but I have been afraid that they are still able to monitor me, so I'm very careful now about how far I go and what I ask of them.

S: *What do you ask of them?*

J: I ask them if I will ever leave and if my child is truly gone.

S: *What do they say?*

J: They are very sad. I can feel the sadness off of them. I don't need to have them tell me to know. It hurts for them to tell me because they have been communicating with me my whole life.

S: *Your child is now in the spirit world. Can you communicate with her?*

J: No.

S: *Why?*

J: I'm not sure, I think I'm too distraught to allow myself to break down that wall to do it. There is too much of a blockage to communicate. I don't think my child understands what has happened and is caught in the in-between. And it is very hard to break through there.

S: *How do you know this?*

J: This is what I feel from them. It seems there were many that were caught like that though.

S: *Tell me more about that?*

J: They died very quickly and they're still not aware that they are dead; they are very lost and confused.

S: *What do they think happened?*

J: They think they are still alive. They haven't processed that yet.

S: *What do they do there if they still think they are alive?*

J: They kind of just wander around looking to make sense of it, but it's so hard to do from that perspective. If I put myself there for a minute, it's very confusing. It's like someone telling you right now that you're dead and you don't believe it because you feel very alive.

S: *Is there help on the other side when something like this happens?*

J: There is, but if they are not believing that they have transitioned, they will have to stay in that place until they are ready to accept that.

S: *Do you get a sense of how long that took for them?*

J: It was different for every single one of them. For my baby, my little girl, it took quite some time because it's harder for the little ones sometimes if they are searching for something, especially if they are searching for something that they can't find on the other side.

S: *You talked earlier about the experiments that they did on you. Are there any others that you remember?*

J: They did many things that felt very cold and scientific. I feel myself strapped to a lot of tables and they also tried something with a lot of orbs around me.

S: *Tell me more about that?*

J: They put me into an orb, and I float a bit in the middle of it using some type of an anti-gravity device.

S: *What was the purpose of that?*

J: It does something to your genes; it can go in and tell about your genetic history. They were trying to find out about my genetic history. They wanted to know why we were on the other side of the planet, and they think they can figure this out by looking at these markers.

S: *Are they able to figure that out?*

J: What they figure out is that we all come from the same place, we originate from the same planet. Their seeding and our seeding are from the same planet. Even though there is diversity in the way we look, that was just environmental.

S: *Would they do any other experiments on you?*

J: They would do some other experiments with waves, with the water, where they would try to submerge me in it to see if the isolation of the water would get me to instinctively start using my skills, my gifts. My gifts never felt like anything different to me until these people came into my life. They would try to hook me up to these other devices and shock me and shock me over and over again. I can remember my teeth chattering, my teeth just chattering and biting off a piece of my tongue and tasting the blood. They did as much torture as they did experiments. Because as many experiments as they did, they really did not get the answers that they wanted. Even though they did learn a lot from me, the more I was successful in hiding how to communicate with these originators, the harder it was.

S: *Let's move ahead to another important day as a prisoner in Atlantis. What do you become aware of?*

J: I see that there is a terrace on one side of the bridge. They have a restaurant out there where it seems very affluent people come to eat lunch. It's very fancy, very elitist.

S: *Tell me more about that?*

J: There are waiters with big trays with what looks like seafood on ice, and something like champagne. The bottles look bigger and they're green.

S: *They're bigger?*

J: They're bigger than a regular bottle of champagne.

S: *What are you doing there?*

J: I feel like I'm there and I'm making a scene. I just came out of the water and everyone is just looking at me.

S: *Why?*

J: They're not sure what I'm doing there. I'm running.

S: *Why are you running?*

J: I'm trying to escape and it's the middle of the day. I seem to have swum there.

S: *Where did you swim from? Do you get a sense?*

J: The other side of the bridge. I went up there and jumped off. I was being chased by someone and they were looking for me. I felt like I was going to get caught anyway. I felt like I was never going to be able to leave but I tried it anyway. There are dogs there looking for me now.

S: *There are?*

J: I see them up on the bridge with the officers; they smell me.

S: *What do these dogs look like? Can you see them?*

J: They're black and grey and very fierce looking. I've been able to scare people enough to just keep getting away from them.

S: *Why are people scared of you?*

J: They look at me like a side show of a carnival. I'm different from them and they know it. They look down on me because I'm not Atlantean, and because of this, they feel that I'm beneath them.

S: *How would you describe yourself there?*

J: No more than thirty. I'm desperate. I have very curly hair and a grey streak that was in the front has grown wider. I have some wrinkles around my eyes and my face looks very sallow and yellowish because I have not seen the sun in a while. I'm very sick and tired looking, with dark circles under my eyes. I've become very thin and weak. Swimming is very hard, there was something under the water. When I jumped in, I realized that there was something under the water that allowed for me to breathe.

S: *Tell me more.*

J: There seems to be this cart, like a roller coaster that would go from up on the bridge and take people down into the water where they could tour what looks like an underwater world that people could visit. It's a way for people to entertain themselves.

S: *They would take a cart?*

J: You could take a cart underneath the water and when you entered the water it would be scary like you were crashing into the water, but once you were under, you could breathe. They had done something to the water. They created some type of oxygenated process where they used a machine, and they poured these bubbles into it. It made it so you could breathe.

S: *So, you can breathe under the water?*

J: Yes, I see this was almost like a tourist attraction; they would usually go for a few hours at the most. They would swim and visit this underwater area that had some buildings and an underwater garden.

S: *Is there anyone there today when you go there?*

J: There were a couple of younger people and some children. Their parents are there, but it's hard to tell under water.

S: *What do they look like under the water?*

J: They look like they have blond hair, very light- colored skin, but they seem scared of me as I jump into the water and they swim away. I only glimpse at them for a moment because I try to swim and get up past this restaurant.

S: *What happens next?*

J: They stop me when I get up to the other end of the bridge. They have guards blocking both directions. The water underneath is part of a circular moat. If I were to jump into it, it would bring me back all around to the center part of the city where I was being stored.

S: *There is a moat surrounding the city?*

J: The moat not only protects the city, but it acts almost like a center piece to show off the wealth and power of Atlantis. There is also a second moat surrounding again the next circle of land and that is their reservoir for drinking water. But the first moat is where people come to experience the novelty of breathing underwater.

S: *What happens next? What else do you notice?*

J: There is a lot of commotion and they are following me around. They will never let me leave there. They have told me that I will never leave, that there's no point in even trying, that I will never get far enough. Even if I were to escape, there is nothing left of my home; my home is gone.

S: *It's all gone?*

J: It's all gone, and I know they're right because I watched it wash away.

S: *Tell me more.*

J: This is the day I realize that I will never leave. I will never leave alive.

S: *Is this the first time that you tried to escape?*

J: This is the furthest that I get, jumping into that water.

S: *How were you able to get away and jump in?*

J: There was a woman that was doing an experiment on me and she made a mistake. She was supposed to lock me in this tube-like container and then go right to the processing room to pull the levers to begin the experiment. The experiment she was doing on me was kind of like an x-ray but for the whole body and it would tell you very detailed specifics down to the ventricles on the body. It wasn't just for bones, it would recreate almost a 3D image of my body and recreate it in a hologram for them so that they could see what was going on inside of me, even down to the synapses that the brain was firing off. She forgot to lock the door of the tube when she said she was going to use the bathroom.

S: Tell me more.

J: I kicked the tube open and was able to get out of the building and just started running. It probably brought more attention to me that I was running. Had I taken a moment and maybe used some material to disguise myself, I probably would've gotten further, but it was so quick and there was so much commotion, there was no plan. But I realized then that they will never be as careless as to let that happen again. There is nowhere to go; it just seems like the end of humanity.

S: Tell me more about that.

J: I had never heard of another culture outside of our own, except for the tales my grandmother had told me of blond ones that they had heard of. And then when we finally met them, we had our empire destroyed.

CHAPTER 15: THE JUDGE

In February of 2020, I was invited to participate as an assistant for a QHHT class hosted in Miami by Julia Cannon, daughter of Dolores Cannon. I was thrilled to have it held so close to my home in the Florida Keys and could not wait to work with other practitioners on their regression techniques. During these classes, the students take turns regressing each other so they may experience new concepts and strengthen their craft. The practitioner who was assigned to practice on me was named Sherry. Sherry had traveled from out of town but felt a strong connection to this area of the world. Sherry was not the only one in our class that felt this pull; it seemed many others were drawn here, not fully understanding why. As we began our session, it became very clear to me why so many of us felt this energy calling us to it. It seemed that we all had our roles in these ancient civilizations, and I was re-discovering my own. Below is a segment of my introspective session with Sherry.

SH: What do you become aware of?
S: I'm in a brick stone building or something made out of stone. It's a building high off the ground, maybe twenty stories up. There is a view of another brick color wall or a stone wall from the window, and behind it is the view of the water with the sun shining onto it.
SH: What color is the water?
S: Like a greenish white. It looks like it's been churned a little bit, like the wind has blown the water around there.
SH: Tell me more about what it looks like inside this office building?
S: It feels a little stuffy in there, warm and with lots of older books that have big bindings on them on the wall next to the window. There are big books piled up on a desk too. The books look very old. It's not very tidy and it's a little dusty. I'm an older man living on my own, it looks like.
SH: Describe yourself to me?
S: I'm shorter and I have missing hair on the top of my head, grey tufts on the sides, sideburns that grow from the sides of the hair down to my face, light skin and light eyes, very large pores on my face, and a large nose that you would see on an older gentleman.
SH: What are you wearing?
S: A white shirt that has a collar with the top buttons undone, a pair of very fine linen, like a very soft, soft blend of linen trousers. They're soft but heavy enough to keep me warm. My shoes are a reddish-brown kind of leather and they are well crafted. They have almost a wooden slat on the bottom. These are not just basic shoes; they look like they were made by someone who knows what they were doing. I also have half-moon glasses on my face.
SH: What about your office? Could you tell me more?
S: There's a lot of burgundy and red in the office. I'm very fond of that color.
SH: Do you work there with anyone else?
S: There are others who work in the building, but no one else works in my quarters except for a very young secretary who works with me. She takes care of me in small ways. Sometimes she gives me food or tea, and she keeps very good track of my schedule and appointments as well as my health. She feels like a family member, but this is not my child. She was brought in

to help, to learn the law.

SH: Is there anyone else that you work with?

S: Yes, there are two. They have their separate quarters on the same floor. They are down the hall. It is a long corridor, a very long corridor with a golden wood colored floor that has been highly polished, and there are cream colored walls that have the same colored wood as the chair rail and molding. There are also very ornate light fixtures that hang down that are very prismatic.

SH: Is there a purpose for them?

S: They are very special crystals that are supposed to bring clarity to those who look at them, and it is a feature of the justice quarters.

SH: Are there any other features there?

S: There are a lot of framed documents on the walls. They are in a language I've never seen before, a lot of very strange markings. They seem very official, like these are very old important laws that have been passed.

SH: What did the frames look like?

S: They are very big and gaudy. Some are brown, some are gold, some have bits of red edging to them to make them look very prestigious and important. They look very old and protected in the glass frames. These are very well-known laws and rulings that set the standards of our society very early on.

SH: How do you spend your days?

S: I spend my days with two other people. They are both older gentlemen like me. There is a shorter man and a taller one. The three of us spend our days going over cases, of what to do with the people who had been mutated by the scientific experiments and vaccines that they had been doing there.

SH: What are these experiments that they were doing?

S: There were many experiments that changed many people in ways they didn't understand and didn't expect.

SH: How?

S: Some people would take on animalistic qualities. There were many different experiments and alterations to the DNA. One of the earlier reasons for these experiments was an attempt to make people stronger or have other animalistic abilities, especially for the warriors. There were also illnesses and diseases for which many vaccines were developed. The side effects of these experiments and vaccines did not show up until the next generation of babies were born mutated in ways that would create an ostracism in society towards them. This would often lead to them breaking laws and committing crimes in order to survive, or out of insanity or mental deterioration because of the process. Our job, for the three of us, was to consult each other in how these people should be treated and what would their fates be now that it had gotten to this level.

SH: You are judges?

S: Yes, we are working together in our older years to help solve this problem because our government is not sure how to handle these people. If we should take them in and allow them to continue being Atlanteans or if we should send them all away and start up a colony for them somewhere else. We are the deciders of who stays and who goes.

SH: Tell me more about that.

S: There are some that we deem fit to be kept here because they have only been slightly altered and it is just a physical difference that people have to adjust to. The ones that have been physically and mentally altered are sent away. They are sent off; there is an island where they send them to. We have been told that they take care of them there and that they have a facility to help them adjust, as well as food there for them.

SH: Where is this island?

S: Off the coast of Atlantis out into the Atlantic Ocean. It seems like the perimeter of the shoreline is about ten miles around.

SH: Where is this located now? Is it still there?

S: No, it's under the ocean. It was too close to Atlantis when it exploded. The rising waters rose up over it and washed it away.

SH: Where would that be now if you could look at a map?

S: It would be close to where we are now; the closest land mass would be the Florida Keys.

SH: How do the three of you start working together?

S: We all worked in different areas before the ruling was made to figure out what to do with all the human-animals. We all worked within the legal system and rose up through the ranks, all three of us. I worked more in the capacity of domestic issues, things within the home that affected people. My other co-worker, the taller one, worked in something more criminally based and was exposed to a harsher side of the people of Atlantis. He was a bit more jaded towards the people because of his experience. It was a hard job for him to do. He had difficulty dealing with the same offenders constantly not being rehabilitated and the failures of the society to not be able to rehabilitate these people. He felt the system was not set up correctly to deal with them. For the shorter man, it was a family profession. It was one of the higher positions to take in the government, almost equivalent to the Supreme Court, but with only one goal in mind: to house and sort these genetic mishaps. As the crisis grew and more children were being born carrying on these genetic traits, the problem grew, and it seems for years we undertake this. This is by far our biggest and last project. It is very tricky because there are many who do not deserve to be forced out of Atlantis.

SH: When did these genetic experiments start?

S: It was before my lifetime when the beginning of the experimentation started. The experimentation continued through my youth, and in my middle ages the first groupings of these children were born. Now they are all in their thirties and the full effects have become known.

SH: So, it was an experiment gone wrong?

S: Yes.

SH: And all of you had the job of deciding who would stay or who should go?

S: Yes, we were all fair judges, and we were all greatly deceived. We were told that the mutated people would go to an island and be taken care of. However it was a lie; it was a death sentence to go to the island.

SH: How did you find out?

S: We decided to take a trip to the island in my final years as a judge. We commanded to go. We were all very, very powerful men. When we got there, we found nothing, just a shell of a building.

SH: What did this building look like?

S: It was a type of stone that looked like it had been bricks that were molded together. They were grey and stacked all around in a pattern. There was no roof left to it, it had been there for so long. Tens of thousands of people had been sent there. We had spent years, almost every day during these years going through the files and deciding the fate of so many people. It wore heavy on all of us. The three of us got to a point where we started to question if this was even something that should have been done. Did we do the right thing in separating them? When we got to the island and realized the whole truth and what had happened to these people, we came back with a great fervor, a vengeance to fix it. And when we got back from the island, they politely explained to us that they were retiring us and no longer needed our services. Knowing how tight the system was in Atlantis, it was like a dictatorship with a thin guise of democracy over it, we didn't have a chance to change what was happening. This desire to help stayed with all of us for the rest of our lifetimes, to help those who have felt like they have been thrown away. We knew the truth of what happened to those people, and what Atlantis did to people. They were always trying to achieve something they couldn't understand, and that was their greatest downfall. They were trying to make an inner connection, but they couldn't do it. They began to sacrifice the humanity in people for it, and it created a cycle of destruction.

SH: Were you able to save any of these mutated people?

S: Yes, we did save many as a result of this decision making, the ones they didn't take to the island. The Atlanteans would soon start to experiment with the genetically mutated humans and create advancements in their society because of them.

SH: OK, let's move to the last day of that life. What is happening?

S: I see that my heart can't take the devastation and gives out. I die of a heart attack.

My experience in Miami stuck with me and naturally left me with more questions. It helped to explain my once unexplainable desire to help others that could not help themselves. I also realized that I had a closer role in this story than I had previously understood. I knew I needed to find out more about this lifetime and find out more about this island where they used to bring the mutated people to, especially since I live in the Florida Keys and in my session I saw how close it had been to where I live! I needed to get to the bottom of it, so I worked with Jen again to go deeper into my past life in Atlantis. Using a keyword and asking to speak directly with the Subconscious, Jen was able to view my past existence and find out more about what my role had been.

S: Could you scan my lifetimes and find a lifetime where I lived in Atlantis as a judge?

J: I see you. I see that lifetime. What do you want to know?

S: Could you tell me about the people who were mixed with animal DNA?

J: There were many mutated people. I see now a race of people who were like cat people. There were many reasons for this, but one of the reasons was because there was some feline DNA that was extracted in order to make people more spry and able to maneuver the way a cat does. I see them finding something in the brain that allows them to complete a study that uses a liquid that doesn't freeze but freezes things it touches. There are also mutated frog people that seem to have a conductivity to them because of their skin changes, and they are able to use this energy and direct it. And this begins some of the work that will lead to the destruction of Atlantis.

S: *Tell me more about that?*

J: This will begin the building of a new energy system that will take over, and many generations later will be the same energy system that will be manipulated and turned against them. It will create an ancient nuclear reaction and expose the entire civilization. I see you, though, your childhood was very scientific. You were taught to study and you were educated from a very early age by your father and tutors. Your father was very insistent about what you should be studying. It looks like you spent your childhood in front of books studying what you were told to study. I see you sitting alone in front of a window that has many small panes divided by panels of white wood. You look very isolated and your mother wasn't very available to you; she had her own things going on. It looks like you didn't have any siblings; you were an only child.

The window Jen described from my Atlantean childhood reminded me of the same windows I recall from my youth in this existence. The small panes divided by panels of white wood that she describes always brought to mind a strange feeling of isolation in my childhood. While my current life was different in that it was made up of loving parents and siblings, I had once again been influenced by my father to find my way into academics, yet it was never where my true passion was. My early days as a student brought about a deep sense of unworthiness and left me believing I was not capable of doing anything correctly. As I transcribed Jen's session and re-listened to the information, it became clear to me as to why I have chosen to relive that experience from my past life in Atlantis. I had constructed a pattern in this lifetime to allow me to confront and lay to rest many of the traumas I had carried with me. With this recognition, I felt as if I had a new freedom and understanding of my current lifetime on a grander scale. I could see how many of my relationships have been affected by these existences, and I felt validation on a personal level for something I did not realize I had been seeking. My awakening did not go unnoticed, as family and friends remarked on a change in me as I healed on many levels. From this deep healing, I began to feel the confidence I had been denying myself for too long grow within my body and mind. I was excited with my new development, and even more excited for what this could mean for my QHHT clients who carried similar past trauma from Atlantis.

S: *Was my father in that lifetime my same father in this one?*

J: Yes.

S: *What did I look like there?*

J: You have very blue eyes, and blond hair, but straight eyebrows that go straight across without a lot of definition. You wore a rougher, thicker type of shorts and a lighter billowy top.

S: *Did I marry there or have a family?*

J: You were mated or married at one point and she died early in your relationship. You never remarried.

S: How did she die?

J: There was an illness associated with a pregnancy. It was early in the pregnancy and it was a blood disease that they couldn't fix.

S: They couldn't fix this?

J: No, these were earlier days before Atlanteans are able to cure everything.

S: Tell me more.

J: Atlantis starts off very advanced from all the technology that they came with, then it dips, and they lose things over the generations until it hits a point again, closer to the end of its reign when the technology goes through the roof. They are able to regain and reconfigure a lot of their old technology again. It comes back around. They also use the technology to do different things than they had once done, so it creates a whole new set of reactions within society.

S: Was I born when it was dipping?

J: When you were younger it was almost at the very end of the dip, and then in your middle age it just takes off, but it's too late for your young mate, your wife at the time.

S: Tell me about her.

J: You were very fond of each other, but it wasn't a deep undying love.

S: What was it like to live in Atlantis at that time?

J: In your lifetime there it doesn't seem to be the greatest place to be, seems like a time of big change. And it's about to enter into a phase that will lead to its destruction. The people could feel that, the end of an innocence.

S: Had the Sphynx already been created there?

J: Yes, that was their outpost, the end of their territory and claim to the river.

S: Do they have electricity?

J: There is energy that is tapped into, but the sourcing looks different. It's like it's already in the walls, already there and when you need it to turn on you can just lift your hand up in a certain way and the light will come on. And when you wave it in a different way the light will dim down. However, it's not a single source, like a light bulb, the whole room lights up; the whole room is wired to it.

S: What about the modes of transportation?

J: A lot of people walk where you live because it is the central part. There are moats around the center. You seem to walk a lot around the water's edge there. The water is very clear and still able to support the growth of things around it. There is also a walkway that surrounds the whole inner moat on the side of the city. It has docks and places where you can bring boats up to.

S: What do the boats look like?

J: They are older, wooden looking ships, very basic ones because this isn't a large area of water. Smaller boats here are necessary.

S: What do the docks look like?

J: They look like a type of floating concrete.

S: You said I like to walk around the water. Do you get a sense of how long it takes to walk the whole inner ring?

J: It takes about three hours to walk around the entire inner ring at a fast, brisk pace. You do that a lot in order to make your decisions. There was a special type of sandal that would wrap around your foot that had a base that when you put your foot into it, it stuck and molded to your foot. It was a special sandal that was customized to the wearer; it created a lot of support and bounce. This was good for people like you as you got older; it created less resistance and less issues with joints. It created a bounce to your step almost. You seem to walk there often with the other two judges that you worked with. It looks like there was also an area up on the roof top where you would go as well. There was a lot of gardening around this structure that you worked in, and you were also adjacent to a big dock by the water where people would gather.

S: *What would they do when they gathered there?*

J: They would watch the boats sail. It was more of an overlook point.

S: *Could you tell me more about my law chambers?*

J: There was a red silk pattern in the wall behind your desk and some white, it looks like ivory almost, and lots of dark furniture. There was a window that overlooked out on to the water, the moat. The water is wide; the moat is about a half of a mile wide.

S: *Where is the ivory from?*

J: From the ancestors of elephants or something similar that have been hunted into extinction.

S: *Is there anything in particular that you notice that seems interesting or important?*

J: As I look at your life from this perspective, I see that you attend lavish parties there. They look very grand.

S: *Tell me more about that.*

J: You and the other judges would attend. You were considered an important person there. The parties were grand, held in grand halls with very large structures and extremely high ceilings. You can find the remains of halls that resemble these still in Egypt today.

All of this information Jen accessed seemed to add up perfectly to what I had begun recalling during my session in Miami. I understood as well why things in my life were the way they were. I wanted to find out more about the island off of Atlantis where they sent the mutated animal people, and so I inquired with Jen's Subconscious.

S: *Could you tell me more about the island where they took people who had side effects of the experiments?*

J: The island is to the southwest of the capital where your office is. It is a little colder on the island during some of the months because it's a little further south than where you live. It's very desolate, except for the abandoned building. The wind can just roll through there; it's very windy sometimes and there is a cold wind that just comes through. There is a clearing all around this abandoned building, a very big rectangular cut clearing where it's just open space. It looks like dead grass grows all around it, like a brownish yellow grass that's just dry, but then in the distance there are a lot of oak trees.

S: *What happens when I go visit this island with the other two judges? Could you tell me about that?*

J: You have on a coat, something made of an animal that keeps you warm. You're very tightly bundled up in this while you're waiting on this ferry that is crossing all of you over from the capital to the island.

S: *Tell me more about the ferry and what it looks like on the inside?*

J: The ferry has a large opening in the back that allows for cargo to be brought onto it as well as many people. The ferry does not have seats on it. There is nowhere to sit. It seems to be made out of wood mostly.

S: *How is it powered?*

J: There is a type of steam engine inside of it, a steam power, or something similar to steam, and a compression of water that powers it. It looks like it takes the water around it and propels it through and heats it, and uses that water to propel the boat so it doesn't require a secondary fuel, like a gasoline or any type of liquid fuel like that. It does have a conduit on it that moves the energy force and propels the water through it.

S: *Could you tell me more about that?*

J: It is like a magnetized energy creating a current. It's magnetic.

S: *What does the conduit look like?*

J: Two large rectangular blocks separated by about four inches and the energy that is created by the two of them being placed right next to each other is then vacuumed out and channeled into a smaller container that looks like a beehive, a cylindrical oval shape made out of metal, either copper or gold. And then from there it uses that to allow pumps to suck the water in and create that steam.

S: *Does steam come out?*

J: No, it has a bit of a different mechanism that propels out into the water underneath. Traveling on this ferry is very cold and quiet. I see that the three of you are traveling to the island today and are very set on seeing what is on this island. None of you are happy; it's uncomfortable not to have anywhere to sit as you are all older.

S: *How long does it take to get there from Atlantis?*

J: It takes about two and a half to three hours to get there so it's a long, cold ride, but it's a sunny day, just windy and cold.

S: *What happens next?*

J: You can see the island in the distance as you get closer and your first thought is where are all the people; where is everyone? When you approached the ferry to get on it, they at first weren't going to let you go because the drivers of this ferry knew what happened to the people who were going there and they had tried to stop you. But while you were on the boat they were radioing, communicating with people in your government telling them you were on your way over there.

S: *How did they radio?*

J: They use something similar to a Wi-Fi blue-tooth signal that is sent out through the air; it does not require a wire transfer.

S: *So, the Government was aware we were going?*

J: Yes, they were aware, and they were trying to come up with answers, lies to try to cover up what happened. And when you arrived there is a huge moment of I told you so. You had a feeling there was something happening, there is a lot of disbelief. The other two that were with you were blaming one another. You are still standing around trying to process where all of these people could have gone. You know of thousands and thousands and thousands who were sent there, and where are the traces of them? Where is the food you had allotted money for and the treatment and the medical treatment?

S: *So, we allotted money for that?*

J: You did. When they first organized the program, it was a humane program they said, and you believed the island was a place that people could go to in hope that they could find a normal life there despite their issues, but it was just a death camp. There is not a trace of any of these people, they were all disintegrated. I can see their bodies just disintegrating into ashes in front of me.

S: *Did they kill them?*

J: Yes, they were turned into dust with some type of a ray-like light. The light would absorb all of the moisture in their body so all that would be left is the dust. That's why you couldn't find a trace of the bodies. **They were all around you, but they were disintegrated into the dirt that was beneath your feet.** And it was windy and very dusty when you arrived at the island and you couldn't understand why your lungs were getting irritated. You were coughing and you walk around the rectangular area of dead grass that is around the empty building and then you go inside the building and it is empty, and you wonder where everyone is. Are we even on the right island? And then you notice the dead grass. The grass has died because the soil is actually the remnants of people and that caused the grass to die because of the high levels of carbon, carbon from their bodies.

S: *Do we figure this out?*

J: You have a very strong instinct here of what is going on. You are very hard to fool and all three of you are very astute. You know that you have been tricked, and that these people are dead. You're just not hundred percent sure of how they were able to pull it all off around you. Every shipment of people they bring in, they evaporated and never told you. They don't keep anyone alive to tell any tales, and it is too far away to swim anywhere from there. The mutated people are all gone.

I have had many clients describe the island in their sessions. Sometimes they describe the building with a roof in its early days, but it is always remembered as an abandoned building. It makes me wonder if it was ever used for what they intended it for. I have also had many clients recount losing their mutated children; most of the time they are reunited with those same children in this lifetime, but I understand that many people are here to clear this trauma. I have also had a few clients' Subconscious explain that the residual effect of these mutated people is still flowing lightly within our genes. The effects are very rare; however, some people are still born with gills, tails, and webbed feet, a result of these ancient experiments and not from an evolutionary mistake. What is also interesting to me is the power of hearing or reading these stories. In the QHHT class in Miami many students in the class had similar experiences in their regressions, even some had strange and spontaneous healings from uncovering this lifetime. One student reported that she had always had a strange affinity for cats and felt different her whole life. She had also developed a strange cough that amazingly disappeared upon hearing this story. But what I realize and what I have learned through sessions is that many who read these words will heal on levels that they did not even know existed. With all of this information I was compelled to understand more and to uncover what happened once the judges discovered the mass slaughter of Atlanteans. I asked Jen's Subconscious to look further and see where this trip to the island leads the Judges.

S: *What happens after we discover this?*

J: The three of you get back on the ferry to go back to the capital, and you discuss amongst yourselves what you are going to present. Because the short one brings up that now that we are the only three people who know the truth, how do we present this without ourselves ending up dead. If they've orchestrated this on this level all around us, then why would three people stop them from keeping it a secret. But you all agree that you must tell the people what is going on. There must be a way. You are all old and have lived your lives, and the last good thing that you can do is allow these people to know the truth about what has happened to their relatives and to stop it from happening again to anyone in the future.

S: *What happened when we arrived back at the capital?*

J: They force you into retirement. You try telling people, but they don't care. You all refuse to send more people there, and the leaders of Atlantis do not want this to get out, so they strike up deals with all of you to retire, to quietly go off and to have your lives. You are all outraged by this. At first you say absolutely not and you strike up a deal where they do end sending people to the island and you will retire in exchange that there is no more harm done these human hybrids. You orchestrate this deal. You were able to get that island shut down. During this time the leader of Atlantis actually had a child that was born with a strange type of genetic anomaly that gave it cat-like features.

S: *The leader of Atlantis?*

J: Yes, the leader of that time. The mother of that child had had a procedure done using the genetic treatments when she was younger and she did not herself have any alterations, but her eggs did. And the child was born with a slight genetic mutation. You were able to talk sense into the leader by telling him that this was not the way you would like your own child to be treated, taken away and removed from society. And they were able to relate to you in that sense. You convinced them to create a system within Atlantis that would deal with these people. They started to find a benefit from them and started to use them to their advantage. The leader was able to see that his child had a strange intelligence when it came to things such as crystals and conductivity, and they realized that they had been killing off the answers to their problems. And from then on, they changed the system, and they utilized these people and found ways to keep them, but only within their own kind.

S: How did they do that?

J: They created a building in which they would test them. It's a very large building on the outskirts, far away from the capital. And they would use these Animal People and test them to see what kind of special gifts and talents they had. They scientifically began to develop new technologies based off of how these people were able to compute things differently because their brains had this different genetic makeup.

S: *What kinds of things could these people do with crystals?*

J: They could easily take them in their hands and hold them up to their heads and tell you the messages that were inside them. And they could also use them to create an energy that would come out of the palm of their hands and this could stop things. It could move things, and also lift things up and down.

S: How did they figure out that they had these abilities?

J: Instead of killing them, they studied them and noticed things that they did to survive because the conditions weren't excellent conditions for living when they first arrived in this new situation. It takes many, many, many years for this experimentation to become something fruitful, and you will have died before you see anything beneficial come from it. You are not around to see the developments they will find and how they will use them to better themselves. Once they find something that is good for them, they will use it and not destroy these people. When they were just a burden to the Atlanteans they were easily discarded, but once they found use in them, they were protected. However, these people were never ever integrated. They were never able to feel that they were part of this society, and they always felt that they were ostracized and on the outskirts because of who they were.

S: Did they stop with the genetic testing after that?

J: No, they continuously found new avenues to create with what they found. I see a variety of different areas of medically treating people and treating animals, disease-wise, growth-wise, and using their innate abilities and developing those. It was all eventually destroyed and forgotten at the end when everything sank. When everything sank, there was nothing that could have truly survived except for shards and remnants.

S: Is there any reason why I live in the Florida Keys close to where this island was?

J: You live on the closest point to where you died in that lifetime. A part of you is still under the ocean waiting for you to complete and share this information, and when you get this out for others to read, this part of you will finally sleep.

S: What about the mutated people that died on that island? Are a lot of them walking the Earth today?

J: There are more now that have been reborn than we have ever had since the incident occurred, since the sinking of the continent.

S: Do you get a sense of why?

J: There has been a block until now because of the closed mindedness we have had, and we did not want to see a repeat of the torture of these people. It wouldn't have been good for them before now to know of their ancestry, but they have allowed themselves to understand now.

S: Why? Why is it good now to know about where they came from?

J: **We have hit a point now where the consciousness is open, and we are breaking away from judging and labeling, so it is finally the right time for these memories to awaken**. There will be people recognizing this because they will have a natural affinity with animals, especially feline animals and reptiles. There were a lot of reptilian and feline splicing in the genes.

S: Why?

J: They had looked for feline attributes for agility and disease control. They had found something in the skin with reptilian-DNA for warriors, to create a second skin that would be more impenetrable in battle.

S: What about the people that had this genetic mutation in their previous existences? Do they carry any benefits into this life?

J: Yes, they have many abilities from those lifetimes. Some of them have an ability to use crystals intricately and very specifically.

S: Can they use them the same way as they did before?

J: Yes, and it seems the feline-induced DNA could control this skill the best. There were also people who had gills that allowed them to breath out of their neck; they were also very good at the crystals.

S: What could the people with gills do?

J: They could use crystals and channel them through their body and could send out waves of golden energy, and this energy would go out and calm people around them. When they would do this to people, the people would suddenly just become very docile and very calm, and very open to whatever they were proposing.

S: How do people now know that they were one of those people?

J: Some people that were once these people in the past have a special affinity to a certain animal, a very deep affinity to them, where they would almost prefer to be around that animal than people. And that will be one way they will recognize this. They will also find that this information creates an opening in their mind and allows for a feeling of justice that will quiet the injustice they have felt and acquired for thousands of years.

S: What was the purpose for these people to have been mutated and then discriminated against?

J: The purpose was to show how people are treated differently by society, and that a society will turn on themselves when they exclude those who are different rather than be inclusive of differences. We are seeing that in our society now, and that is why this book needs to be written.

S: Why?

J: Because we are seeing the same inequalities happening to people of different colors as we did when we had people of different colors there.

S: Is this a cycle that goes on and on?

J: Yes.

S: Tell me more about that.

J: It is a seed of injustice that was planted when we first saw differences in each other. When we would see others that looked similar to us, we would not fear them, but when we saw others that looked different, we would.

S: Where does that come from?

J: It goes back to the origins of fear that came to this planet. We are now at a point evolutionarily where we are removing the outer layers of the fear that have held us back. While the full fear can never be removed because it has its place here, and it's made its home here, and it has just as much a right to be here as the rest of us, we no longer need to use fear as an excuse to separate ourselves from our true identity. For thousands of years we have projected this fear on anything that does not look as we would want it to look, and we have sent people away hoping this would then keep us pure, but it does not. It is the integration that is key to everything, and the need for equality amongst all. That is the only way that we will progress past our past and transition into the next level of consciousness. This is what holds us back, and it has cyclically held us back. It is time for this fear to be shed, and that will begin now.

S: *Are we headed in the right direction?*

J: Yes, it is millennia in the making. Discrimination has played its role and sowed its seeds, and now it's time for the weeds to be ripped up, and it is time to grow something useful.

S: *What do you mean when you say move into the next level of consciousness?*

J: The next level of consciousness will be one of equality where we no longer look to judge, or to fear others based on our differences. But we will begin to veer into each other's minds and feel who a person is rather than see what a person is. We will begin to use our intuition about people more. We will begin to subtly communicate with each other using this internal voice rather than our eyes and our judgement.

The information the Subconscious provided was enlightening and exciting. How great it would be to live in a world without discrimination, where we would truly see one another for who we are and not what our appearance looks like.

S: *Was Atlantis always scientific?*

J: For the most part and from what I can see Atlantis has always been a scientific, cold place that was founded by someone who was also very cold and very distant. When I first arrived as a prisoner, the medical technology was very similar to what ours is right now. Our medical technology is very similar evolutionarily, the path of becoming curious and opening bodies to understand how they work, leading to innovations in medical science. It seems very similar, very much on the same track.

S: *Did you see any other types of healing modalities?*

J: I did not see it. This place did not seem to foster that. The energy that they start to derive from the animal people was something they had a hard time believing was possible at first. The use of crystals was something that was purposefully kept from them from the very early beginnings of Atlantis.

S: *Why was the use of crystals kept from the Atlantean people?*

J: The leader did not want them to know anything that would allow them to have too much free will or choice.

S: *Why?*

J: The first leader had this mission of building a replica of what he had on the home planet that he missed so much, and he had no issue with using these people to do this for generations. And the more he kept the truth from them about their true origins and how to use these energies and crystals, he believed the longer those in power in Atlantis would reign. He believed that the key to his reign would be to keep the people in the dark. As I review this, it is very similar to what is happening with our current society.

S: *What can we learn from this?*

J: There is only the work that needs to be done within the individual, nothing that needs to be done in an outward motion to convince others. Everyone's path has been planned. The most powerful thing is writing because writing has the ability to help people with a different mind-set look at something and analyze. Writing gives the ability to go back and simmer on things and slowly change one's perspective on things. When things are spoken and it is too accosting, it shuts people down because they are too busy formulating a response against foreign ideas. But writing has the power to change beliefs.

S: Now it seems like there are so many similarities between the ancient civilization of Atlantis and our current life now?

J: That is why **it is relevant and important that we begin to uncover what took place there for us all to learn from this. And to move away from this predictable future because we understand now where it will lead,** if we continue to treat people in such a manner. There is also a correlation between the vaccines now with the human DNA being injected into babies, and the experiments back then.

S: Could you tell me more about that?

J: There is a specific type of preservative that goes into the vaccines now that has begun to cause alterations in the brain and was not put in there necessarily for any form of benefit. The vaccines you have now are similarly affecting the genetic code through the brain, but the difference is it is not animal derived. The medical community in our current society has been disgraced. It has fallen from its true goal of healing and has been intermingled with the consumerism and mass marketing of our pharmaceutical industries and the financial benefits that come from the teaming of these two together. There is a very definite link of repetition in history here. **History repeats itself until we have completed the lesson.**

S: What happens after we complete the lesson?

J: We proceed into the next lesson. There are eternal lessons. If there weren't any lessons, there would be nothing, and nothing is nothing.

S: Are there any lessons that we have figured out in the past?

J: There have been many millions through the ages of lessons we have overcome. But we are at a very big turning point for equality amongst all, and that is why we are seeing the remnants of this surfacing again, to remind ourselves of our history and our origins and how we have been doing the same thing for thousands and thousands of years. It is time to learn the lesson and move on. There will be in the next three generations a group of people who are more advanced as a result of their exposure to your vaccines and different forms of energy. And the most important is the mindset of those educating the communities. The communities will change, and we will have a different approach to how we relate with each other that will show these new generations a very clear-cut path to ending this cycle. We're on the very end of it and we're being given the chance to end it, and we can either choose to end it and allow it to trickle out in the next three generations, or we will choose to continue and perhaps in the next ten thousand years we will uncover once again the same pattern and look to correct it.

S: There is a choice?

J: There is always both destiny and choice.

S: Is there a divine purpose for the vaccine experiment happening now?

J: It is an altered consciousness that allows those who have been affected and afflicted in a negative. It is not negative, in a... well it is a very different approach to the human mind... and that was needed now. It should only be construed as though different parts of the mind are being opened. For some, that is the only way a person can handle the reality around them, with the mind being opened that way. We have labeled this affliction derived from these vaccines as autism, but for some, autism has derived genetically from vaccines that have been given to previous generations. Where it did not surface in one generation, it came out in the next.

S: What about the future of autism?

J: There is fear in that area, but in the long term the results that come from those that have chosen to be afflicted will be outstanding and we will uncover many advances in our society as a result of these people being affected in this way.

S: What type of advances?

J: Definitely on the scientific level. You can already see this with the savants that there will be channels opened in the mind that will allow new ideas to come through. There will also be many advances in learning equality because many that chose before birth to have autism are here to teach equality.

S: I had a teacher tell me that her very non-verbal autistic students are telepathic?

J: Yes, many that are non-verbal could easily communicate amongst each other and may be doing so in a very highly cognitive way that we are not even able to trace at this point.

CHAPTER 16: REMEMBERING THE EXPERIMENTS OF ATLANTIS

I have worked with many people who have shared their confusion about past life memories of being an animal or animal-human hybrid. They brush it aside because it does not add up to anything they have seen in the current world around us. I have always felt there was something more to these interesting memories, and then I met Erica.

The circumstances surrounding Erica's session seemed like just a coincidence at the time, but I have learned time and time again there are no coincidences. Erica was from upstate New York, just recently divorced, and felt a strong unexplainable need to go on a trip to the Florida Keys. She thought that she was just embarking on a vacation until she arrived in the Keys. For some strange reason, as soon as she was halfway across the Seven Mile Bridge that connects the middle to the lower islands, a strange emotion took a hold of her and made her cry. She described that she felt as if a memory was resurfacing, a memory of a different life. She was compelled to call a friend of hers from home and was given the suggestion of seeking out a QHHT session while in town to get to the bottom of this odd feeling.

My sessions are normally booked a few months in advance. However, I had just been notified of a cancellation and was surprisingly able to fit her in at the last minute. When we met, Erica felt that she wanted to try a QHHT session to release trauma that she had experienced through continuous failed attempts at IVF, which she felt resulted in her recent divorce. What she found during her session was eye opening.

S: *What do you become aware of?*
E: I feel as if I'm looking at a city from the water. I see people bustling around tall, tall buildings that are very beautiful. I feel as if I'm a mermaid.
S: *Could you describe what you look like?*
E: Sort of like a cross between a fish and human. My body looks blue and scaly, but I have arms and hands.
S: *What is happening? What do you notice?*
E: I sense that I was so free and now I'm trapped.
S: *How did you become trapped? What happened?*
E: People acted kindly to me and I trusted them, and then I was caught in a net. They trapped me and put me into this small, very small cylindrical tube. There was barely enough room in there for me; it was so uncomfortable. I feel like they kept me out of the water a lot too.
S: *Why?*
E: They wanted to do experiments on me; they would take out my eggs!
S: *Why did they take out your eggs?*
E: It feels like they wanted my eggs to do experiments with them. I know this seems really strange, but I think they were using my DNA and splicing it with human DNA. They did all kinds of experiments on me!

S: Tell me more.

E: Sometimes they would take me out of the tank and see how long I could stay without water. It was so painful. Other times they would just shock me until I would pass out. Ugh, they are not nice people.

S: Tell me more about them? What do they look like?

E: I can't tell what these people look like because they are covered in some sort of gauze, even their face is covered. They look like scientists doing experiments, but on me. It looks like they're experimenting on all of my eggs.

S: Do you notice what they do with your eggs?

E: I feel like they're trying to understand what I am as well as mixing parts of me with full human DNA.

S: How do you feel about this?

E: I feel used and wonder why they feel they have a right to do this to me.

S: Could you tell me more about how they trapped you?

E: I felt as if I was friends with these humans at one point. I was very curious about this populated place and one day I allowed the people to see me. The people seemed so happy about this that I kept going there. I could feel their joy when they saw me and so I wanted to keep going for them. I know that there was genuine joy, especially on some of the children's faces when they saw me. It was like seeing a deer in the woods for them somewhat. What I didn't realize was that some of the people that lived there had other motives. One day I showed up and they took me. They took me into a dark cold place and placed me into a tube. I could tell that there were other beings in tubes next to me, but I couldn't see them. I could only feel their intense pain.

S: Tell me more about that?

E: I felt that they were being experimented on too, these other beings. It was not a nice place.

S: What happens next?

E: Eventually I just gave up. My heart gave out and I died from a broken heart, from all the terrible things that they did to me.

S: Ok, just leave that scene and that life and now from a different perspective do you get a sense of what the purpose of that lifetime was?

E: It was to learn acceptance and to help the humans remember magic and love.

S: Tell me more about that?

E: There were little children that needed me. It helped those kids to feel valid in the magic of their imagination, and it helped them to open up and eventually pass this down. No matter how crazy things got in their society, there were still some people who believed in magic, even if it was through stories because those stories came from something real. The stories kept that door open. It kept that stream of magic alive so that the people who did see it or feel it could connect with it. And now I can see that there were a lot of people who didn't see me, but all it really took was one person. In a way I was a beacon for those who felt different. Those stories that were passed down because of me helped them remember. It helped because it was the seed that was planted that kept going in the subconscious even after their civilization was destroyed.

S: *Tell me more about that?*

E: I don't see the details, but all I know was that this place is called Atlantis now. I don't know why they were destroyed but it feels like they could not continue their society because of what they were doing.

S: *Anything else you notice that seems interesting or important?*

E: I see that my father in this life was one of those little kids who saw me in that lifetime. I see the effect that it had on him then, and the effect that my being his daughter has on him now. I see that I'm back here again to continue to open that channel.

S: *Why did Erica experience failed attempts with IVF?*

E: They were never supposed to work. They were meant to trigger a response and memory of the lifetime as the captured mermaid in order to rebalance her karma. **Karma is not a punishment but a choice to do things differently.** Erica is not meant to have children in this lifetime, and she knows this, and during her treatments she felt the same violation and abuse of her own will. The treatments were meant as the catalyst for her to start her inward journey and the catalyst for her to seek help. Now that she has received this information all the trauma will leave. she is noticing a big difference already.

S: *What is she feeling?*

E: She feels as if she has just been set free; (sigh of relief) this is one of the reasons why she had to come all the way from upstate New York to the Keys.

S: *Why did she need to come to the Keys?*

E: Because what happened in Atlantis is still there. The energy of it is still there and it faces out in this direction of the Florida Keys and it is like a tide that brings that charged water here, like a basic conductive agent. The Florida Keys are one of the closest points to this energy.

S: *Is there anything you want Erica to do while she is here?*

E: We brought her here to be close to this water so that it would be a charging to the soul, reactivating those memories to make sense of what happened.

S: *Does she need to go into the ocean to have this charge?*

E: She just has to go to the ocean to feel that expanse, but it would be extremely beneficial for her to submerge herself in the water. It would be a natural activator.

Erica emailed me a few weeks after her session reporting that she felt a new freedom and happiness that she had never experienced before. She explained that this was a result of her session and the understanding that came with it. I began to see why clients like Erica had to come to the Florida Keys. They were coming to regain a piece of themselves lost in Atlantis. The red crystals responsible for the island's end must still be in the water somewhere, and this is one of the closest points to feel them. After Erica's session I was curious as to whether or not the legends of mermaids were true. I had heard on many occasion people talking about mermaids in early Atlantis, so I decided to work with Jen to see what I could find out.

S: *Could you tell me about the legends of mermaids in Atlantis?*

J: They are not legends; they happened as a result of seeding the planet. There was a sprinkling of them put in the sea to see if they would do well.

S: Did they?

J: They didn't do as well as those on land, but they were better at hiding away. They were better at avoiding the colonizers and were a bit more rebellious.

S: So, they were able to hide away from the colonizers? Does that mean they didn't advance like humans?

J: They evolved in their own way based on their needs and their environment in the ocean.

S: I heard people often talk about mermaids during the time of Atlantis. Was that true, was it common to see mermaids?

J: Not when I lived there, but earlier on the people who settled Atlantis first had a lot of contact with them. They cooperated with humans at that time to help feed one another, but only after the first colonizers were gone and before the new colonizers began. It was just them with a very simple-minded group of early humans. It was more of an animalistic group of cooperation in trade.

S: What happened to the mermaids?

J: There is just a very small population of them left in underground cave systems in order to avoid the excess of boats and pollution around them. They travel to many places because they migrate seasonally.

S: Anything you find interesting about them?

J: They are more fish-like than human, but they do have humanoid characteristics. They have eyes and a nose and stuff like that. They do not have cities; they live in caves.

S: Do they ever surface?

J: They do, to be curious.

S: How do they communicate?

J: They can use echolocation and they also have their own language.

S: Do you get a sense of what it sounds like?

J: It sounds like that of a porpoise.

S: Are they similar to humans in any other way?

J: Yes, they have families; they work together and live together in pods.

S: Tell me more about early, early Atlantis. What happened?

J: There was a big fight that happened amongst the crew that first came to colonize it. There was something that just went wrong. And they had decided to move on and ascend themselves. They did not want to continue with the experiment.

S: Why?

J: Too many of their crew experienced tragic deaths and it took a toll on their mental wellbeing.

S: What happened?

J: One of them snapped and killed four of their people there on the island. The others had to stop him and kill him to keep him from hurting them. And they all were too shaken from that experience and felt too much guilt to continue. There were three that left and decided to ascend.

S: How did they do that?

J: They transported themselves through the stone circle system that you would see in Stonehenge. They traveled out of that place and went into a different dimension, instead of traveling to another stone circle. Because they did not go back to the home planet, their bodies transformed into an energy force.

S: Did they colonize before they left?

J: They had started and had two hybrid children who had been born to the people, but the children didn't make it.

S: When did the Atlantis that you were a prisoner on get started?

J: That was later, when I lived as the Commander. One of my crew left me and went to that island. He used the stone circle to go through the chasm and when he got there, he realized that the earlier colonizers left all their equipment. He was able to use a lot of that combined with our technology that he recovered from the ship when he starts his new civilization.

S: What happened to the beings that ascended?

J: They are still there. They are still beings of energy.

CHAPTER 17: ATLANTIS CALLS ITS SOULS HOME

The more I pieced together the story Jen was detailing in her sessions, the more the universe responded by sending clients to my office with past life experiences of Atlantis in their sessions. I had started to understand that the energy of Atlantis could still be felt here, and in a way it called to these people as if to bring them back to this energy to finally break free from their past trauma. I have noticed a correlation with many of my clients who come seeking healing for their eyes and regressing to past lives in Atlantis or Lymuria. It is almost as if they need to recount this specific past life experience to find clarity in this one.

Robert came to me for a session because he wanted to know if he could heal his eyes. He had suffered from astigmatism for as long as he could remember and decided that he wanted to try Dolores Cannon's method of QHHT. It was no surprise to me when Robert began to describe a place that sounded all too familiar. This is his session:

S: *What do you see around you?*
R: Buildings, lots of buildings that look a little different because they are made of different materials that I have never seen before.
S: *How would you describe these buildings?*
R: They are greyish blue large buildings that have see-through windows, but the materials are a lot stronger than what we have today. You can't break these windows.
S: *Interesting, what else do you notice?*
R: I see lots of clouds, and the sky is a pinkish, purply color, grey almost. There looks like there is smog sort of or grey clouds, maybe something is burning somewhere around me.
S: *Do you get a sense of what could be burning?*
R: No, I don't see anything from where I am looking, just the smog.
S: *What else do you see around you?*
R: Lots of stores that look like they sell very advanced electronic tools.
S: *Is there anything interesting that you notice?*
R: I see a green sign with letters that look like the Pi symbol almost. It isn't exactly that symbol, but something similar. That is the only writing I see.
S: *What about modes of transportation? Do you see any?*
R: Not right now, but I see people walking.
S: *How are these people dressed?*
R: They seem to have grayish clothes out of a material that I don't recognize at the moment.
S: *Look down at your body and see if you have feet there?*
R: No, I don't. I'm just observing this place from above before I decide if I want to be born here. I'm not in a body yet.

S: What do you decide?

R: I decide to do it.

S: How long before you decided to be born did you watch this area?

R: It would be hard to explain, for about twelve human years before.

S: What made you choose that place?

R: I'm planning to live a hard life; this will be a challenging life in Atlantis.

S: What makes this life hard?

R: There are a lot of people here who are very mean and self-centered, which makes this place more challenging.

S: Tell me more.

R: I forget this information when I'm born, but I start interacting with mean people when I start going to school. Well it's not exactly school, just kids I socialize with.

S: What is school like for you there?

R: You just go into a building and get the knowledge; it's hard to explain. There aren't any teachers or a class.

S: What does that feel like?

R: It feels like your mind is really fresh, and fresh with new ideas. It feels like your head gets cold before the knowledge is put into it.

S: Could you tell me about some of the knowledge that you have gotten?

R: It's very scientific, a lot of probabilities, and learning about what to do in case things happen. *S: What do you mean?*

R: Scientifically preparing for things; we always prepare.

S: Is there anything interesting that you do to prepare?

R: No, I don't like it here. I want to go far away from this city. I live alone, deep within the city. S: Tell me more about this city?

R: There are very tall buildings and a system of moats surrounding the city. There are different classes of people according to what ring of the city you live in.

S: Where do you live?

R: I live in the second outer ring; the inner ring houses the elite and wealthy individuals.

S: Do you have a job there? What do you do during the day?

R: I help clean things like restaurants and stores. I have a tool that sucks in dirt and trash and it disintegrates it once stuff gets sucked into it.

S: Where does the trash go?

R: It is just obliterated; it turns into nothing, there is nothing left behind.

S: Do you like this job?

R: It's OK. I'm getting paid.

S: How do you get paid? What does the money look like?

R: Like coins that are grey/ silver with nothing on them.

S: *Ok, let's leave that scene and move ahead in time to where something important is happening. Be there now. What do you become aware of?*

R: I'm old, not really old enough to die of old age yet, but I had left the city for a little while and now I am coming back to try to work and find a place to live. I find a job, a better job than when I was a kid.

S: *What kind of job do you find?*

R: I find a job where I look around to see if there is trouble, and if there is, I just report it to somebody.

S: *Have you found any trouble?*

R: Yes, just some fights. Most of the time it starts with someone saying something. Today it's a fight where they are using tools that they shouldn't be using to fight one another.

S: *What type of tools?*

R: Tools that could destroy one another.

S: *What happened after you saw them?*

R: They put the tools away after they saw me because they knew they would get in trouble.

S: *How do you feel about your job?*

R: I like it, and I like my house. It's a small apartment in the city. This city is very big, and there aren't many ways to get to the mainland.

S: *How do you get to the mainland?*

R: The land bridge. The water there is blue, very blue because it's shallow like twenty feet deep and you can see fish in there. I see a bunch of grey fish that look like they have blue tails.

S: *What else is around or in this city that looks interesting?*

R: There are boats; some are very long boats and they're used to catch fish. They have motors that have a different type of power.

S: *Is the motor on the inside or outside?*

R: Inside. It looks like the motor uses some type of steam that powers it. I've never seen anything like that before. The city looks old yet in some ways very advanced and very beautiful. Oh! I do not want to see this! I don't want to see!

Robert began crying as something was obviously upsetting him.

S: *What do you see? What is happening?*

R: It is just horrible, horrible what people do to one another here. I see a man who has been experimented on; it is so incredibly sad.

S: *What happened to him?*

R: It looks like he was given animal legs as if they were sewn onto where his old legs used to be. He looks like he has just walked out of the place where they did this to him, and he is dying in the street.

S: What happens next?

R: It looks like someone quickly takes him away so that others do not see this.

S: Do you know why they did this to him?

R: No. I see that they did many terrible experiments on people here that I just do not want to see.

S: Is there anything else that you notice that seems important or interesting?

R: I've moved ahead in time now and I'm just old and ready to die.

S: Tell me more.

R: I'm in the hospital. It's is one of the biggest buildings in the city; it has many rooms, it doesn't have to be that big, but they make it that big. They can easily cure people of everything.

S: Do you get a sense of how they do that?

R: I just know that they've figured out how to cure people of anything except old age.

S: Are there any doctors there? Do they assist you?

R: I've left my body now and my soul is leaving so I can only see their heads. But from what I see most of them have brown or blond hair. There are three of them. They just wear regular clothes and not the doctor's outfits you see today.

S: You said that they can cure people of anything. Could you tell me more about that now as you have a different perspective?

R: Any physical issue the person may have can be cured at this point. They don't really cure anyone if they lose a limb or anything like that because people can do that themselves now.

S: How do they do that?

R: They just regenerate it using energy that they harness from somewhere.

S: Do you get a sense of how they get this energy?

R: It feels like it is extracted from some sort of person or people, but I really don't know who or how they get this.

When Robert was saying this, I felt it matched up well to what I had heard from others about the so-called Animal People of Atlantis. His description of advanced technology and human-animal hybrids was intriguing yet traumatic, and so we continued to find out more about his experience from a different perspective. I always find it interesting to know what happens after a person has left their earthly lifetime. Below describes what most people recount, or similar to what most recount during their sessions.

S: Now that you're leaving that lifetime, do you get a sense of what the purpose or lesson for that life was?

R: It was just to challenge myself and to be brave. But now I understand that that is why I blurred my eyes in this lifetime. I did not want to see! I didn't want to see the crimes against humanity then, and so I made sure I wouldn't see them clearly this time. But now I realize what I did! I feel like it is being released; I feel my eyes tingling.

S: *What is happening?*

R: They are healing!

S: *How do you feel?*

R: So good! Now I feel like I go into the sky and it feels amazing!

S: *Tell me about it?*

R: It feels like a sense of complete belonging, love and weightlessness. I just pass into the next world.

S: What does that world look like?

R: It is that in-between sweet spot; it's very light in appearance and feel. There is just an airiness about you, an unhindered glow around.

S: *Do you recognize where you are?*

R: Yes, it feels that you are just above everything else looking down in a very warm suspended way.

S: *Do you feel as if you have a body, or no?*

R: No, I don't feel a body, but I have a face, a head in a way. I feel that it's very wispy...what I have for a body.

S: *What do you like to do there?*

R: I like to soar above cities and swoop in, and just fly around and look at things from way up above.

S: *How does that feel?*

R: It feels exhilarating.

S: What else do you like to do there?

R: Everything. Eating here is interesting. You can taste anything you'd like, but there's no physical putting things in your mouth. If I thought of a chocolate cake, I could immediately taste the sensation of a chocolate cake going down and the warmth of the gooeyness and the sugar, and the memory of that would come right to you.

S: *What about people? Are there other people that you spend time with?*

R: If you want to see them, you can, and if you would like to be alone, you can just be on your own.

S: *Are there any dwellings or things of that sort?*

R: I don't feel a need for any kind of dwelling. It doesn't feel like it's necessary because houses just shelter you from elements that don't affect you at this point.

S: *What about classes? I've heard many people talk about the classes they take in the in-*

between life.

R: Yes, there's school. You go and you study what you've done in the past and you study what you would like to do in the next life. Then you go and you make plans for what you would like to accomplish and you figure out what other things you can intertwine into it, to make it a really interesting life. You also figure out who you want to interact with next time as well.

S: *How often do you go to this school? Can you tell me more?*

R: It depends on what level you are on. If you're in a place of mourning or you have just left a body, you may want to stay up here where I am for a while and just be by yourself and take it all in. And when you are ready, and you feel that you are ready, you can go process things from your life through one of the schools. During this time, you can also go see if you would like to find a side project and help others.

S: *Tell me more about that?*

R: You can guide and help others. You can look after them. Sometimes you are sent to do that even though that is something that you weren't looking to do.

S: *Tell me more. Who would send you?*

R: Sometimes there's just a more perfect assignment for you when you are in that in-between place, and even though you can't see it at first, by the time it's over you have gained something beneficial from it. There is a connection between you and the sender. There is more than just one big sender; there are several different aspects of it working as one.

S: *Could you tell me more about that?*

R: It seems like there is this big giant capsule of different energies that are very old and very wise and operate sort of like a brain almost where it can make things happen all over the place without you even realizing it. And you're not really aware, but you are in tune with it; you are an extension of it.

S: *How do you feel towards these big energies?*

R: The same way you would feel towards your child or parent that you love very much. You feel that you are a part of it, a continuation of it, and there is a comfort there. There's a familiarity and a very deep sense of belonging to it, kind of like sitting on your parents' sofa in your pajamas. There's no awkwardness about it; there's a connection.

S: *So, you feel as if you are an extension of it?*

R: A very specific extension of it, yes.

S: *Could you tell me more about that?*

R: Picture a big thing of slime that you can hold in your hand… and part of it could drip down to the ground, but you're still holding a big chunk of it in your hand. You are an extension like that. You aren't part of the big part in the hand anymore, but you're dripping down towards something different. And when you're ready, you go back up to the big clump and you share what it is that you did when you were a drip.

S: *So, do you share what you did in that life with everyone? Is that what you mean?*

R: It feels like it is a collective sharing so others can learn from you, but it's never the same as when you learn it yourself. The sharing from others can give you good ideas for how you would like to precede in your future existences. In that way you always have something to work with, new ideas, and new concepts to breakdown and jump off of and leap from.

S: *Is there anything else important or interesting about what you are looking at?*

R: That I have never truly been alone. I am always loved, and I am much more than this physical body.

At this point I asked to speak with Robert's all knowing, all powerful Subconscious to find out more about why they showed him this lifetime and more information about his eyes. This is what the Subconscious said:

S: *Robert said his eyes were healed. Is this correct?*

R: They healed energetically, instantly, as he understood why he had blurred them. The full physical healing will take a week to complete.

S: *What will he notice?*

R: He will feel a slight tingling sensation during the day, but most of the healing will take place at night while he sleeps.

S: *So, in a week what will he notice?*

R: He will notice full and clear eyesight returning to his vision. However, one eye will always be darker, and one will always be lighter.

S: *Why?*

R: To always remind him that the dark and the light he sees are still the same thing.

S: *Why did you show Robert that lifetime? What did you want him to understand?*

R: To see what he has been so afraid to see. He doesn't need to be afraid anymore.

S: *Could you tell me more about that?*

R: He was afraid to see the similarities of this current society and the one in Atlantis, but he needs to understand that the negative has just as much a role to play in the growth of a society as the light does.

S: *Does he understand this now?*

R: Yes, and his eyes will always remind him of this.

Robert woke up out of the session and noticed a slight clarity to his eyes and a lightness in his body. He emailed me a week after his session reporting that his eyes were in fact healed. He stated that he no longer needed to wear glasses and that one eye is now darker than the other, a reminder of his healing that he loves.

Below is another session with a client named Cathy. Cathy came in for a QHHT session because she was curious about the process and was eager to learn about her past lives. Once Cathy was gradually led into a theta state of hypnosis, I could not help but notice the same technological advancements she described of the ancient life she was regressed to. Below is an excerpt detailing the finery and sophistication she witnessed during her session:

S: What do you become aware of?
C: It's cloudy here; no, it's actually grey for some reason. It looks almost like smog.
S: Oh, tell me more about what you notice around you?
C: It looks busy with people working. But I'm confused because the people seem very advanced and I feel this was a very long time ago. I notice that the windows are made of a very tough material, tougher than glass. Also, wow, there is a lot of technology here.
S: What technology do you notice?
C: Well it looks like some people actually have flying carpets!
S: What do they do with these?
C: It looks like they use them for transport.
S: How do they do that?
C: Alchemy, magic, they use magic. They create all sorts of innovations here.
S: Tell me more.
C: They seem to have watches, and crystals that power things, and lots of ways to make life easier for everyone.
S: Could you tell me about some of these ways?
C: They had elevators and things you wouldn't think that people would have then. Technology that shouldn't have been available to them, but they had it and they were workers. They worked with their minds so much, they did a lot of tinkering. There were great inventors there.
S: Could you tell me about the inventors?
C: Yes, there were many of them, but it was too much. They never erred on the side of feeling anything, they just put all of their efforts into innovating their technology. And they did not ever, ever cater to their emotional bodies, but there was one particular inventor who could alchemize gold.
S: How?
C: He would concoct it and make it, and then he would use the gold to cover things. The gold is beautiful and all around here.
S: Tell me more about that?
C: There are golden objects everywhere, golden staircases even. The gold was created and alchemized, and I see golden cutlery, plates, and jewelry. But it's such masculine jewelry, like masculine watches and rings.
S: You said the people had watches. Could you tell me more about that?
C: Yes, they were the first humans to use the invention of time.
S: The same time that we use now?
C: Yes, they invented the watch and were the first humans to use what we know as time

now because they wanted to make sure they were using it all productively. They were very productive.

S: How did they have all of this knowledge?

C: We had knowledge and technology that was given to us from the extra-terrestrials that seeded us.

S: How was it given to you?

C: The very early Atlanteans were given this information in many different ways, and most of the technology was stored and found under the chambers of the Sphynx.

S: What was under the Sphynx?

C: Technology and information. It was put there so that there would be access. The information and technology grew and grew amongst our society. It grew and grew, and it was too much.

S: Why was it too much?

C: We just advanced in that area without advancing within ourselves. There was no balance. Everything was for work here, nothing here is for pure joy or fun. Everything here is very masculine, like many people here eat big turkey legs and have big over the top feasts. The feasts though, they look very luxurious with very big cups of wine, were not for fun but because you earned it, and you worked so hard.

S: Let's leave that scene and move ahead in time to the last day of that life. What do you become aware of?

C: It's just an average day. I go to work. Nothing seemed unusual. I had no preparation for what happened.

S: What happened?

C: All of a sudden the noise of an explosion threw me out of my body, and that is where I witnessed the intense explosion that blew everything up! There was no preparation. I had no idea.

S: Did you feel pain at all?

C: I don't think so. One minute I was working, and the next I was out of the body. There were many of us just looking at one another in disbelief.

S: How did you feel?

C: Just confused for a second and then a realization of what happened. Atlantis had been destroyed, although I'm not sure how.

S: What happened to all the technology from Atlantis?

C: After the continent was destroyed, the knowledge and innovations went back into the collective. A little was physically saved, but most of it was destroyed with the island.

S: Is there anything else that is important for Cathy to understand about this lifetime?

C: She needed to see this to release the trauma that she has stored and brought back with her over the span of many lifetimes. This was the right lifetime to understand this life and the trauma has now been released.

Cathy's story reiterated to me the magnitude of how many individuals are affected by this ancient trauma. After her session, I was left with a lingering thought: What effect could it have on the world around us if people could find healing from this primordial wound in this lifetime?

CHAPTER 18: THE VIRUS, VACCINE, AND QUARANTINE IN ATLANTIS

In April of 2020, the Corona virus quarantine had been going on for about a month. My forced seclusion allowed for much work to be done on this book and inevitably, more questions began to surface. I wanted to know more about the virus of Atlantis, and what correlations there were to the world unfolding around me. I was able to try a new way of working with Jen during this time that allowed for her QHHT session to be held outside with plenty of distance between us. Without a glitch, Jen was able to slip into a hypnotic state once her keyword was uttered and began to bring clarity to my questions. Here is what we found:

S: *You said before that there was a virus affecting the people of Atlantis. Could you tell me more about it?*

J: The virus caused an overthrow of their society; it nearly caused the leader of Atlantis to lose his position. He went in search of a cure for the virus because he was about to be overthrown and was desperate to maintain his position.

S: *Why was he about to be overthrown?*

J: He had lost the belief of the people because it had been going on for too long. It had been going on for two to three years at this point, the virus.

S: *What type of virus was this?*

J: It looks like something that would cause vomiting, excessive vomiting, and eventually it was like a cholera. You would dehydrate and die from it.

S: *Do you get a sense of where this virus came from?*

J: Looks like it was something that escaped from one of the laboratories. It was something that they were studying that left on the back of a scientist one day, accidently.

S: *You said it had gone on for years, and many people died?*

J: Yes, the population was heavily hit. It looks like they burned most of the bodies and spread the ashes into the air, causing the sky to look almost grey.

S: *Were there any precautions that they took to prevent the spread of this virus?*

J: They had a massive quarantine of people, a very big quarantine. It's the emptiest place, very creepy, but very militant. It's very rough during that time, almost like Hitler's Germany.

S: *How did the people who were quarantined know what was going on?*

J: They had a system that spreads information into the homes of people who live in these cylindrical buildings, especially in the inner most parts of the city first, and they are able to spread the messages through these buildings very quickly. At first, until it becomes an issue people are very unaware of it, but there was a heavy measure to protect the wealthy and influential.

S: *How did they get rid of the virus, or did they?*

J: It looks like it starts two or three years before they come to seek us out on Lymuria, but it seems like it's a few more years while I'm imprisoned that they continue with what looks like a vaccine that is administered to the people.

S: Could you tell me more about this vaccine?

J: It was a mandatory vaccine that was given out about two years after my arrival on the island. It was derived from an animal source and there was something within the animal's DNA that they were able to replicate it with. In order to give it to so many people they needed to pull something from these animals in to make enough, and to give to everyone, and that was what messed up their processing. It looks like an incision was opened up on the arm, and then the vaccine was smeared in and then a covering was placed over the arm to keep it in there.

S: There wasn't a needle?

J: No, I don't see a needle, but rather a small incision and then something like a Q-tip that rubbed it in almost like a plaster being rubbed over it to keep it inside.

S: Did this vaccine work as far as protecting the people from this virus?

J: It had very few side effects at first. It was hailed as a success and it was the cause of a lot of celebration. It took a few years before the negative results started popping up.

S: What were the negative results?

J: Children were being born with deformities; they were being born with things that they shouldn't have been born with, or missing parts of their bodies as a result of this first round of the vaccine. There were deformities and the slight appearance of what looks like a reptilian skin, or strange hair on some of the children, like a fur or a scaling. This is when they first started to understand that there were repercussions of the vaccine. It took a couple of years before the children who were administered the vaccine were old enough to have children of their own.

S: What happened next?

J: It was very unexpected, and it began very quickly. These women were giving birth to children with all of these deformities that looked somewhat animalistic, or arms and legs missing. They quickly looked into revamping this vaccine; it went back to trials. A good generation later they had to readminister the protocols of their lockdown once again because that destructive vaccine needed to be stopped until they came back with a new one. But the new one did the same thing.

S: There was another quarantine?

J: Yes, because they had to stop giving the vaccine to children, the virus found its way back again many years later, but it wasn't as big of an outbreak this time. They were able to figure out how to switch around some of the genes in this virus, and they were finally able to fix the vaccine for good the third time. The third time was the charm, they fixed it then and had no more issues with the vaccines. But from the second time and the first time of administering the vaccines, there were a lot of children who were born with these deformities, a lot of them were taken away from their parents at birth and killed. Others were killed by the families themselves because it became such a stigma to have on your family name. But from the second round were the children that you dealt with in your life as a judge in Atlantis. As they became adults, they learned how they were not welcome in their society, and they were not considered people.

S: So, a lot of the issues with the animal people came from the vaccine?

J: Yes, it all derives back to that.

S: *This sounds similar to what is going on now? Am I mistaken about that?*

J: There are many, many similarities, especially when it comes to the social unrest; it is the same. There is a similar feeling of being used by the system, and being drained of your life force, for a system that does not value you as an equal member of society.

S: *How is what humans are going through now with the quarantine and what happened in Atlantis correlated?*

J: There is the same fear; the same type of isolation that leads to what looks like a new type of development in the brain from this isolation.

S: *Isolation redevelops the brain?*

J: It will cause the brain to develop differently. It's more of a closing in with less distractions around you that allows you to focus inwards and you are able to grow differently as a person as a result.

S: *Could you tell me more about that?*

J: The brain begins to wire itself differently through isolation, and the things that you look to do to appeal to others and to create your place in society are no longer relevant. And so you focus on different things. The focus is more on inner development rather than like a peacocking effort for the development of others.

S: *Is this the same thing that happened in Atlantis, or no?*

J: It is the same feeling, the same environments, and it is our job to avoid the same outcome of the very few in charge at the top turning our world into a very strict dictatorship.

S: *How do we go about changing this?*

J: We have already allowed for ourselves to have a different outcome for this and it is a progression. There is a natural progression that is unfolding, and we are already moving away from that even though it would feel as if we are close to it. The Atlanteans were also much colder than we are now, as we have more of a mix of our qualities from both ancient colonies that let us appreciate the things that we were missing then. We understand the beauty of life. This was never something that was important to the Atlanteans, and when they lost that, it was detrimental.

S: *Could you tell me more about the virus now? Is this virus supposed to trigger memories in the people that went through the virus in Atlantis?*

J: Yes, it was specifically meant to do that. It was meant as a very big trigger. The virus is meant to open people's eyes to look at what is going on around them because life can be very blinding and very busy. This trigger was placed for people to receive the memories that they have forgotten and for them to start putting pieces together about their previous existences and their role in these existences.

S: *It seems as if history repeats itself, and the virus in Atlantis was close to the end of that civilization. Is this the same in our civilization? Are we close to the end as well?*

J: It looks like we're at the end of the old life. We are changing, however, this is not the end. There is a cycle to this; we are all balancing our karma from our lives in Lymuria and Atlantis.

S: *Tell me more about that?*

J: This is a do over. After both of those civilizations were destroyed, we all met in the afterlife to review what had happened and there was so much trauma, so much destruction to account for. With all this karma it was decided that these civilizations would meet again now. We all chose this, and so far, we are choosing differently. We are choosing love, rather than destruction.

S: *I have heard this time period has been called the Great Awakening for years and years. Do you get a sense of why this label has been placed upon this time period?*

J: It looks as if everyone has been living their lives half asleep for a very long time and people have been very closed minded, closed off and very judgmental of each other to the point where we are no longer allowed to be ourselves. And that has become so dangerous and detrimental to our development that if it's not stopped now, we will continue to develop in the way of the Atlanteans and cause our own demise.

I have had many clients in their sessions say similar things, especially about learning to be themselves and to accept others as they are. On many occasions, the Subconscious will tell a client to look deeply within themselves in order to understand what they truly want and not what others want for them. They are also encouraged to look within themselves to feel their own greatness. The Subconscious has often said that it wants humans to know themselves authentically and individually, and that by knowing yourself so deeply, you empower others to do the same. Most humans are so caught up in attempting to be so much like one another but when everyone tries to be the same, no barriers are broken down and no progress is made. For many thousands of years people have been wanting to play small, but this can't go on for much longer. The Subconscious calls this time that we are experiencing "a Great Awakening" as it is undeniable that a shift within humanity has occurred. All around us, because of the Coronavirus and its impact on our day to day lives, people are working towards getting back in touch with their true individual identity, and investing in a future that is more aligned with the wants and desires within themselves. In other words, the Subconscious insists that if you come to understand yourself at a deeper level, rather than follow rules instilled by another, then you will find yourself on the correct path, and it seems people in this world are finally beginning to follow this advice.

Miguel came for a session in 2016. I don't remember the details or why he came for the session. I hadn't even thought about this session for many years until Jen had recounted her memories of a virus in Atlantis. At the time of Miquel's session, I never thought that perhaps he was remembering Atlantis and I don't think either one of us knew that much about this mystical place. However, as the information about Atlantis and Lymuria unfolded in front of me, I wondered if Miguel's session took place during this time. Unfortunately, the recording equipment I used in 2016 was not as good as my current system. The recording was kept on my phone, and most of it is hard to hear. This is a short segment of Miguel's session that I think is corresponding to our subject matter.

S: *What do you become aware of?*

M: I am aware that I'm in a small room made of stone and wood. It looks very advanced yet old, if that makes sense?

S: *Tell me more.*

M: I see lots of things that don't really make sense, like very advanced looking devices, but they are old looking. I'm even looking out the window at what looks like a hovering car.

S: *Tell me more about that. The car is hovering?*

M: Yes, it doesn't look like it's flying, but hovering. I know that doesn't make sense.

S: *What else do you notice around you?*

M: I see my family; we all have to stay inside for some reason.

S: *Do you get a sense of why you have to stay inside?*

M: I don't know; I don't feel like we're in immediate danger, but for some reason it feels like we have to stay inside.

S: *Do you get a sense if you want to stay inside, or do you want to leave?*

M: No, I think we want to stay inside. There is something we're trying to stay away from.

S: *How is your family; are they scared? Or not scared?*

M: Hm... they don't look scared, but slightly worried. Oh, they are worried about catching a virus that is plaguing the city.

S: *There is a virus that is plaguing the city? Is it deadly or not deadly?*

M: Yes, it can be. We are in quarantine.

S: *What has that been like? Has it been going on for a long time?*

M: No, I think a few lunar cycles, not that long. My family is more afraid of our leader, he is a tyrant.

S: *The leader is a tyrant?*

M: If anyone goes against him, he will kill them and their whole family.

S: *Tell me more. You're more afraid of your leader than the virus?*

M: Well, I would say the worry is there for both. But one is certain death; the other has possibilities.

After this segment the recording becomes so low and hard to hear that even when pressing my ear against the phone with the volume at the highest level, I could barely make out anymore. In retrospect, after my session with Jen, I believe that Miguel's session took place in Atlantis during the quarantine, even though he never mentioned Atlantis by name.

CHAPTER 19: THE OLD LEADER OF ATLANTIS

It appeared that the old leader of Atlantis was a cruel and heartless dictator. I wanted to know and understand more about this leader and his role at this time, and so Jen and I worked together to find out more in June of 2020. This is our session:

S: Could you tell me more about the old leader of Atlantis?
J: There seems to be what looks like his need to continue his reign, to continue as leader with a boost of approval and success of his mission, which was to collect and bring our technology back to his people. He would stop at nothing so that he could continue his power.
S: Tell me more about that?
J: He becomes something different when he cannot get what he wants. He becomes very brutal; he becomes a dictator to his people and their approval no longer matters to him. He goes off the deep end during this militant state; he just takes over the country, and it becomes a very dark place while I'm in prison.
S: Tell me more.
J: He goes very crazy when he cannot get the information from me, and he takes it out on his people. He becomes a very evil dictator.
S: How does he take it out on his people? Could you tell me more about that?
J: Anyone who opposes him and his ideals, not only does he kill them, but he kills their entire lineage. The whole family would die, so if it's an elderly person with great-grandchildren, the entire line will be taken out.
S: How would they find out if people went against him?
J: He had his spies and people as double agents working all over. He had double agents on double agents. There were people everywhere who wanted something better for their family at this time. It was a very difficult time, and people were willing to do or say anything to survive.
S: Could you tell me more? What was it like for the people at this time?
J: It was very scary, but they were not emotional people, so it was a feeling of being cold and strict like a catholic school, very rigid.
S: Could you tell me more about the old leader of Atlantis and how he died?
J: I hear one day that he has died. I'm very old and I'm in my cell and it looks like someone slides food underneath the door like they do every day. It's this metal door, and then they don't come back to get it like they are supposed to. And then two days later someone opens the door and lets me out, and I remember the light. The light was so very bright. The light inside my cell had broken, so I hadn't seen light in quite a few days and when I finally saw light my eyes felt like they were burning. They took me and they started questioning me. They were asking me who I was and what I was doing there.
S: What did you say when they asked you that?
J: I couldn't communicate with them; my mouth kept shut. I didn't communicate and they took me somewhere that looks like a hospital. It looks like they were freeing many prisoners there after the leader had died. He had died clutching his chest; it looks like his

heart gave out and he had a heart attack. He did not take care of himself and he was very crazy. He had all kinds of erratic fits, and would go on these long tirades, and one time in the middle of one long non-sensical conversation he was having with himself, he died.

S: So, after he died, they began to release some of the prisoners?

J: They began to search for some of the people who had been missing for years during the regime. It was as if people were suddenly overthrowing the government now that the leader was gone. But they were not overthrowing with disregard, they were overthrowing in a very orderly, very Atlantean way, a very well-organized overthrow is what it looks like.

S: And what about you?

J: The people there were looking for the political prisoners. It looked like they brought me to a hospital or lab room where they would examine you. There was a very cold looking metallic table with lights above it. It reminded me of laboratories they held me in when they would experiment on me. They hadn't done that in quite some time, and it felt too familiar, even though it had been many years since I had last been in that position.

S: I see, and what happened next?

J: I feel like an animal that's being held down, and I'm freaking out because of it. I feel a disconnect going on between myself and these people. I start fighting with one of them and I end up biting one of them.

S: What do they do after you bite one of them?

J: They throw me into a holding cell in this hospital. One of my arms is tied to the bed and it makes the news. My attack makes the news. And when the news is shown, the judge happens to be watching and recognizes who I am.

S: Tell me more about that. What do you mean?

J: There was a young boy that I encounter when I first try to escape, when I leave and jump off the bridge. He and I exchange like a piece of our souls for a second. It was a very strange thing that happened.

S: What happened? Could you tell me more about it?

J: He is a direct descendant of the founder of Atlantis, and even though I had no way of knowing this at the time, that is what happened. There was a meeting of our two souls that connect for a moment. From our ancient ancestors, it was an exchange. This was the judge. He grew up to become this judge, however, we met first when he was just a boy. He hears on the news of the attack and immediately he was intrigued and went about getting control of my case, of figuring out who I was because I look similar to what he remembers, even though I'm very old now.

S: Does he know who you are?

J: He doesn't at the time, but he knows that there is something very special about me and he is different from the other Atlanteans because of this exchange that we had early on in his life. But he covers it up well; they have no idea. They think he is just like them and he blends in well.

S: Do you talk with him after that?

J: Yes, I spend quite a bit of time walking with him at night.

S: How do you do that?

J: There is a special guard that takes us and walks behind us. But it is the only time that they will let me outside to walk. We walk the inner circle of the city. There is a boardwalk, a walk that goes all around the center ring and you can walk the whole thing and we do that each evening with my helper (the young girl) and the judge. Occasionally, I can take a walk in the day if I am heavily guarded.

S: *And this young girl is the one who takes care of you?*

J: She was assigned to look after me after her family was wiped off the map by the leader.

S: *So, you all walk mostly at night. Do you talk about anything?*

J: At first nothing because we are all upset for our own reasons, but it feels like the judge is the first friend I've had in sixty years. It is a very good thing for me. I look forward to this walk. We begin to slowly understand each other as we do these walks every night. The judge has decided to take my case.

S: *Tell me more.*

J: He looks to free me. He looks to do what he can to get me my own apartment in this very high security building so that I can have a window and a place of my own, and I can see sunshine. He wants me to go home, but I tell him that I have no home to go to, and so he looks to make me comfortable while I stay in Atlantis.

S: *You told me about the apartment before. So, he is able to get you the apartment?*

J: Yes, and it's very close to where he lives so they come to visit me and pick me up for these walks. It looks like it's about a year between when I'm released from my cell and when Atlantis is blown up.

S: *So, is the judge alive when Atlantis is blown up?*

J: He dies right before it; he dies from a heart attack it looks like.

S: *What happens to the young girl?*

J: After I transferred all the information that I could to her, and before I helped to blow up Atlantis, the young girl escaped into a chasm.

CHAPTER 20: THE GUISE OF THE NEW ATLANTIS

I was curious about the final days of Atlantis. It appeared that it would have been a celebration of sorts and a start of a new Atlantis after the old dictator had died, so I was curious as to what happened that could have been the catalyst for their destruction. I continued my questioning with Jen to find out more.

S: What was it like right before Atlantis was destroyed, especially for the people who lived there? Did they have a sense that it was going to be destroyed?
J: No, I don't see a general concern about the destruction happening. They were very unaware of their own impeding destruction, and looked like they were actually about to celebrate.
S: Why were they about to celebrate?
J: They felt as if they were about to be victorious in moving forward with their technology as they believed that I was going to hand over the information for the good of the continent. And they acted as if they had changed because they had changed rulers, but they had not, and they had not lived up to a standard that changed my mind. I was about to just let it be and die and blow it up at this point. I see something that proved that it had not changed, that they were still the same savages who killed all of my people.
S: Can you see what it was that changed your mind?
J: The treatment of the young girl who is assigned to me is the beginning of it, but there is more to it. It was the way they used their people in the energy conductivity process. They have enslaved people, and they have enslaved them to facilitate this new technology, and it will only grow further in its system of slaves.
S: Could you tell me more about the slaves?
J: They were the Animal People. The treatment of them was an abuse of the system. This abuse would only grow and grow to fulfill the need of the people who utilized it.
S: You saw this and that triggered you to realize that they were never going to change?
J: Yes, they were turning into a country of people who were enslaved and imprisoned like myself, all of this functioning to benefit a few.
S: There were lots of people enslaved?
J: It was what they considered the humane alternative to the death camps for the Animal People who held gifts, and it looks like they began to purposely manipulate the DNA in certain people and impregnant them with these ova/eggs that had these animalistic qualities, to create these conduits of electricity. It was like a breeding program for disposable labor, but it literally looks like they just suck the energy and the life out of these people and replace them when they die.
S: And these are people?
J: These are people, Animal People, yet they are still people!
S: What were they doing all this for?
J: They had found out how to use a very special type of energy to perfect the human body. The energy adds a health to the body, like a glowing rejuvenation that will allow a person to live a long life and look very young.

S: *Were they able to recreate this with the Animal People?*

J: They could recreate this technology with an animal person conduit, and it looks like they could take an older person and channel this energy into that person and it would cure their ailments and make them look younger and revived. But it would slowly kill the animal people conduits.

S: *Do you get a sense of why it would kill these people?*

J: It was just too much. The energy was just too much that it would overload their systems. It would fry them and short circuit them out. It would create a very...like I could see them... they had their brains zapped and left just stuttering. You could look at their eyes and there was nothing.

The information about these people was hard to take in. It seemed like there was a lot of corruption and disregard for human life there. I wanted to find out more about the walks that Kala had taken during the day to see if there was anything else important or interesting that we hadn't previously covered, so I moved Jen to a time when she was on one of her walks during daylight hours.

S: *You said you took a few walks during the day while being heavily guarded. What were those walks like? What did you see?*

J: The walks during the daytime were very infrequent, but they were amazing. I had this feeling of awe, almost a feeling of a guilty awe. I couldn't help but look around and be impressed with what they created and to find it beautiful. The city of Atlantis was very detailed, lots of detail on the stonework and the facades of buildings, and it was a very beautiful mix of old and new. They had managed to combine the two where it did not look out of place, but more like a mixing, a melting pot of old and new ideas. It was supposed to be called the new Atlantis now that the old leader had died. People seemed very busy during the day as they were walking around me and trying hard not to look at me. They wanted to, but they felt that this was a new Atlantis, and they are not supposed to stare, and I can tell that it is very uncomfortable for people.

S: *So, in the new Atlantis they weren't supposed to stare?*

J: Yes, they felt this new freedom for the first time since the old leader had died.

S: *How did people act in this new Atlantis?*

J: It looks like they reacted in all different ways. For some it was like a midlife crisis, for others they would go out and do lots of crazy things. Some would cut all their hair off and dye it different colors, and feel that removal of who they once were into who they are now by changing themselves completely and very suddenly.

S: *People would color their hair?*

J: Yes, they were making a statement by doing this because some felt they did not want to fit in to the rigid society any longer.

S: *What did these dyes look like?*

J: They were more natural looking and were from things that they grew that had color to them, like beets. It didn't look permanent. It was a removal from the silver blond that most people had there. It was a way of distinguishing oneself from the patriarchy of Atlantis, of this continuing genetic factor of this blond hair. Not everyone had it, but those who did were thought to have been better than others with this hair. They were purer, sort of like the Aryan brotherhood.

S: Really? Could you tell me more about that?

J: This was the original feeling, like the sand in the clam that creates the Aryan brotherhood.

S: What was Hitler tapping into?

J: He was actually looking for the red crystals.

S: Why was he looking for the red crystals?

J: He dreamt of it; he would tap into it in his dreams. He started off wanting to free and help his people, to pull them away from a war that had hurt so many and changed the minds of so many, because of the exposure to the chemicals in the pits. I see him lying on his stomach trying to worm away from this. He wanted to help them, and he began to see these images and this information and then his intentions changed.

S: Why did his intentions change? What happened to cause him to become such a terrible person?

J: The power became too much. He began searching for this red crystal and it drove him insane.

S: Did this power take him over? Why did he want to kill people? How did this happen?

J: He was too susceptible to the thought of people around him. He still cared too much about how people viewed him, and he needed to have this superficial power over them. He could not let go of that and it was the key to his downfall because of using this for the betterment of himself and not for the betterment of those around him. And he saw within it what it could do for him and the power it could bring him. Because of this, it had to be taken away from him.

S: Could you tell me about the symbol of the Swastika? Is this a symbol pertaining at all to the red crystals?

J: This was him tapping into something very sacred during a very stressful time in his life when his vision was taken away from him.

S: His vision was taken away from him?

J: It looks like he had bandages all over his eyes, like he's bleeding from his eyes. During this time, he is vulnerable, and he is given these visions and ideas through dreams. It was believed at first that he may be the one to help free society from creating the situation that had occurred during World War One, but he turns towards the opposite way, towards the destruction and the chaos that creates the change that brings the new thing. And he uses this information with poor intentions; he has lost his mind. He has lost control of his thought process and it has become too erratic, and the power was eventually taken from him.

*S: **What does the symbol of the Swastika really mean?** Does it have a meaning?*

J: This is the ancient symbol that represented the four elements of the Earth combining in a formation representing the chasms swirled all together. The Swastika represented the things we needed, the earth, the wind, the water, and the light, all four combined together to create the circuit to build an underground tube of what looks like molten lava to connect these energies, these portals on Earth from the seedling days.

S: Why did Hitler want a white brotherhood?

J: In his hysteria he does not distinguish between the two civilizations or cultures and sees Lymuria and Atlantis as one. He was picking up on the silvery blond hair in Atlantis and how these people felt superior. That was how he got it all wrong.

S: So, on these walks during the day was there anything else that you noticed that looked interesting?

J: I see the statue of the very first leader of Atlantis, the founder. It is located in the center of the capital. It looks like a man holding a trident. It is similar to what others have imagined Poseidon to look like. I also see the trollies. They looked like a bullet train almost, rounded on the top and it comes in very steep in the front, like a very sharp line to reduce the friction of the wind.

S: There is a statue in the capital of the founder of Atlantis holding a trident? Could you tell me more about that? **What was the trident used for?**

J: It was something he found when he first arrived at the place called Atlantis. It had been abandoned by the people who owned it before him. He found it after traveling through the chasm to get there. It had energy that could be propelled from it; he used it on people because it could immobilize them, but it was never meant to be used on people. It was supposed to be used as a building device. It could suspend, lift, and put things into place. The three prongs were for the circuitry inside of it. It needed to have three exits for the energy to come out of. This was so the energy could be balanced correctly and levitate inanimate objects that they would want to lift into place.

S: How does the trident have this energy in it?

J: Within the staff is a kinetic energy made of an eternal force inside of it that could continuously power itself. It pulls energy in from its surroundings. This energy is something we can't see but is all around and abundant on this planet.

S: Where does the energy come from?

J: It surrounds us. It is in the air we breathe; it is all around us. It isn't far away or up in the sky; it's something that emanates out from the Earth and reaches all around us. This energy would continuously charge the trident as long as there wasn't any damage to the device.

S: So, the founder of Atlantis found this trident left behind after he went into the chasm. How did he know what to do with it?

J: He understood what the device was because these were used on the home planet. The trident was also one of the devices that they had taken with them and then lost during the crash landing into the salt-lake, the quarry. That was part of their equipment that was damaged. But, the new trident that was found was linked to an older time in Atlantis. The people who had come to colonize before had abandoned their project.

S: So, there was a statue of this founder in the inner most circle of Atlantis? What happened to his trident? Did anyone receive it after he died?

J: He lost it somehow. There was a battle with the Mer-people and this trident. They were the ones responsible for taking this trident and the red crystals away from him. They did this because of all the experiments that he was doing on them. Before the founder of Atlantis had arrived there, the Mer-people and the humans were friendly with one another. They also had a mutually beneficial arrangement where they traded. The Mer-people watched in horror as this new leader, the founder, created a hostile takeover of the humans that had once been free for thousands of years. Over the years the Mer-people concocted a plan to take the red crystals away from this dictator. They eventually took them and hid them in these caves deep within the ocean.

S: Are they still there?

J: Yes, they are very deep within the Earth.

S: Do the Mer-people living today still know about these crystals?

J: Yes, it is a large part of their secrecy in interacting with humans.

S: How did they get these crystals and take them away?

J: There was a plan that was created when the founder of Atlantis was distracted, but I can't see it clearly. It looks like he makes a simple mistake. He didn't realize the Mer-people could be a threat. The power this dictator had went to his head. The crystals were taken towards the end of his life. The battle between him and the Mer-people lasted many, many years.

S: What happened to the Mer-people after that?

J: He did things to try to kill them off.

S: What did he do?

J: He would create and detonate bombs into the water to kill or injure them, and the ones that survived, he would torture. He also experimented on them as well.

S: He experimented on them back then?

J: It was very rudimentary compared to the experiments in the later days of Atlantis. It wasn't beneficial to anyone. It was very cruel and unnatural. He would match pieces of bodies almost like he was taunting them. Sometimes he would use pieces of them as bait to gather more of them.

S: Did he fight with them before they took his crystals, or after?

J: It was a slow journey for the Mer-people to gather and hide the crystals away. They took them over time. There are points in time when they are able to take more than a few, but the dictator was very smart to not leave them all in one place.

S: How did the Atlanteans continue to build without the red crystals?

J: The founder lived to be a very old man, and during this time he saw the rise of this city built using his slave labor and the many generations that he created and manipulated quickly. Once the framework was in place for him to build these places, then it naturally flowered out on its own. Much of the technology is eventually lost over the years, and the crystals were taken.

S: Anything else you notice on the daytime walks that looks interesting?

J: The Atlanteans look like ants, all looking down, and it is not the way we walked in my homeland. We walked with our eyes up and open and ready to greet people.

S: What else do you notice about these walks?

J: It is usually sunny, not hot, very temperate, with a white glow to the sky.

S: I thought you said it was smoggy and hard to see the sun when you would look outside of your window?

J: No, the smog was from the bodies they were burning when I first arrived. This has lifted since the virus has been removed.

CHAPTER 21: TRANSFERRING THE POWER TO THE YOUNG GIRL

I was curious to know how and why Kala had given the powers to the young girl. Below is the session with Jen that allowed for clarity on this subject.

S: Can you tell me more about giving the powers to the young girl? How did you know to give them to her?
J: She was the only person who matched my anger towards these Atlantean people. It was on this level that we were a match to transfer this energy.
S: So, you had to be a match on the level of anger?
J: Anger and distrust towards them, to know that it was not going to go to the wrong person. There had to be a connection there. It is overwhelming, the connection we have. And she seems to have understood that this was going to happen.
S: How does she know that this is going to happen?
J: There is a feeling that she has had that was the opposite of the feeling that I had growing up. I knew that it was always going to end with me. She felt that it was going to begin with her. She could not understand why or how, but she dreamt of the place that she would eventually go to as a child. She would dream of this new island that she would be eventually sent to. She had fleeting dreams of it and for moments she would remember, and when she would wake up, they would dissipate afterwards. But the feeling would always be there. It is a very intense feeling. She knew she was going to go to this place, but she had never seen it before.
S: What did it look like?
J: It was by the ocean, but it was not the same kind of ocean. It was green and calmer, like a bay almost instead of rough grey and dark blue water that she had seen growing up in Atlantis. It was very calm and serene there. There was a feeling that everyone knew and appreciated her, and that everyone knew the true person she was and loved her for it. The feeling is more than love; she was a part of their community and lives, and she could feel this deeply, even though it had not happened yet.
S: These were dreams?
J: Yes, dreams of another place. They didn't make any sense to her until she transported herself there.
S: How did she transport herself there?
J: She went through the chasm unexpectedly. She fell through a cavern hole in the mountain that she was climbing. And through this cavern hole she fell through an old chasm that had been built by the ancient arrivers to Atlantis, the first set of arrivers.
S: Was it at all planned for her to fall through the chasm?
J: It looks like every step of it was planned.
S: Why was she able to travel through the chasm? I thought it had to be the Equinox or you had to have the right amount of crystals to travel through this?
J: She had the crystalline structure of the red crystals, like a combination of having some of mine mixed with some of hers. By her holding mine, it allowed her to enter through. And

she did not need the red crystal because her powers were so great.

S: *She had powers?*

J: She had powers that she was born with but had covered up for years so that she would not be thrown into a facility and experimented on.

S: *What powers did she have?*

J: She was a subtly affected cat person.

S: *Could you tell by looking at her?*

J: It was very subtle, and you could only guess by her eyes that something was different about her. But it was not enough to bring questioning. Her powers were kept well within and she was able to push it away for years and did not understand them.

S: *What type of powers did she possess?*

J: She could feel the intentions of others and could see into the possibilities of the future. She could conduct the energy very well and was able to communicate with the other side.

S: *What do you mean when you say the other side?*

J: The old planet, where the information is being stored. She could communicate with them slightly. It is weak because she is not trained properly from an early age because she had pushed it away.

S: *So how did you give your powers to the girl?*

J: The strangest thing is that she does not receive all the powers. She receives certain memories of mine, of the events that have led me here. And when she begins to take the power, she sees what it has done, and she does not want all of it. She does not want the responsibility of that.

S: *What has it done? What do you mean?*

J: The need for the power destroyed my homeland. And she sees that it is going to destroy hers as well, and she is then afraid to take it with her to this new place.

S: *So, what happens?*

J: She takes some, but then withholds the rest. And the rest stayed with me in the afterlife. But she has taken enough that it will guide her and allow her to complete her mission on the new island.

S: *How did you transfer this power? Can you describe the process?*

J: It is strange and exhausting. Once we were sitting across from one another to create a natural circuit, it feels like you are being pushed out of yourself. We did not touch. It was necessary to have quite a few feet between us so that the energy would not backfire and harm either one of us. It was a very natural process, as natural as going into a trance with my grandmother and seeing our ancestors on the other side. It is not a hard process for me to let go of this energy, but a hard process for her to accept it, and she fought it and fought it. She is very traumatized already from the events that occurred already in her family, and to take on such an immense amount of... it wasn't just power, but the memories of what had happened to me...it was a very heavy thing to hand off.

S: *So, it wasn't just power; it was memories too?*

J: The memories had to go with the powers because they are a part of each other.

S: *Why?*

J: The powers that I have are a collection of the energy of the memories of the people who came before me, and it had been passed through that.

S: *Would you say then that reading this book would contain powers if they are reading these memories?*

J: It would contain information that would help trigger the opening needed in a person to pull information and start activating their own powers.

S: *It activates someone's powers?*

J: Yes, the energy from this information will do that.

S: *What happened after you transferred this power to the young girl?*

J: They had taken the girl and they had brought her to the facility on the island where they were going to do many terrible things to her. I knew it was my time to go. I had wanted to go for so long, and I was very eager to go and I wanted her to go as well.

S: *How did they get her and take her away?*

J: They had been watching her for a very long time; they knew who she was, they knew about her. Her grandfather had been making deals with them for many years to keep her safe and to keep them away from her, but he did not understand how powerful she was. And from the government's experimentations on others they understood how powerful she was. And they wanted her power, and they had waited and could wait no longer. They needed her, and they decided to take her.

S: *Wasn't she taking care of you? How did they capture her?*

J: While we were walking one evening, you (the judge), me and the young girl, they pull up behind us in their travel spheres and they grab her and they throw her into one, and it closes and shoots up into the sky and disappears. We are thrown to the ground and knocked unconscious, and when I wake, I know to send word that I am ready to die. I awake with that message. I send word that I am ready to hand over the powers.

S: *Tell me more.*

J: Now that I can see this from this perspective, I see that the girl received the right amount that she needed to receive, and I obtained what I needed to obtain. I would have not been able to perform the explosion that I did without the powers that I still had; it would not have worked. And it would have kept those people in a cycle of imprisonment and abuse, and that is why it worked the way it did.

CHAPTER 22: THE LAST DAY OF ATLANTIS

I wanted to know more about the destruction of Atlantis as many of my clients shared their own story of what had happened in their sessions. The trauma seemed to plague many, and I thought it would be important to dissect and clarify with Jen the final days of Atlantis.

S: Let's leave that scene and move ahead to the last day of that lifetime. Why did you decide that that was the day?

J: It all looks very well planned now that I can see it from this perspective. The timing of it was very intricate.

S: What was the morning like? Do you remember?

J: I was awakened before the sun was up and brought down into the facility and I saw the red crystals that they had. They were on this very tall looking bell jar device, like a silver platform with a column down the middle that looks like a cake display with a glass looking dome over the top of it, but it's not glass. It was something stronger that protects them, that holds this power so that it does not misfire around them. It protects those who cannot channel the energy. They brought me there, and as the sun was rising and I saw the golden glow... it was like a shaded grey golden glow in the sky...once I saw it, I knew I could begin.

S: What did you do?

J: I sent word the night before that I was ready to die, that I was ready to tell them how to use the red crystals in return for the freedom of the young girl. I insisted that I would only share my knowledge if she was released. I promised to show them how the energy worked, and she was traded for myself. But now seeing this from a different perspective, I see that she would not have been freed otherwise. And she had only been superficially given freedom. Once they understood the power and energy of these crystals then they really intended to hunt her down and bring her back to the facility.

S: So how did she escape?

J: She was shown the front door and allowed to leave. And that is when she ran.

S: Tell me more. How did she know to run?

J: It was a memory that I had implanted telepathically to her. It gave her the download of the information and she knew that she needed to leave and go in the direction of the mountain that she could see. And I told her to continuously climb up this long mountain. It was very hilly and rocky, like a wooded path up this mountain. And she needed to continue up it until she saw snow. And when she saw snow, that is when the memory ends. She knew she needs to get to that point where she saw nothing but snow around her. And she travels up the mountain and sees the snow. She is blinded by the snow and there is a hole in the ground that she cannot see, like an incline that leads you into something. It is like a large cavern within the mountain and within the large cavern is where the chasm is located. It was built within this cavern thousands of years before, earlier actually, it looks like hundreds of thousands of years...it was one of the earliest chasms built.

S: Tell me more about this chasm.

J: It was created in this opening of the mountain because the right amount of wind and sunlight charged it and kept it active, yet it was very secluded from view.

S: So, she falls through this chasm?

J: Yes, she falls through and begins this new life.

S: So how did you blow up Atlantis? Could you tell me more about what happened?

J: The new leader of Atlantis comes to get me. He looks like he is younger than the last one. He claimed to be this new light, that he was going to enlighten these people and bring back the golden age of Atlantis before the old ruler had destroyed it. That was how he presented himself. He worked with the old leader though; he was not a rebel that took over.

S: Was he really planning on bringing this golden age back?

J: It does not seem like he is what he says he is. He has been brainwashed so deeply by the old leader that he understands power and he wants this power as well. He is a very two-faced person, and he comes to get me because he wanted to be there when the powers were exchanged.

S: What did he look like?

J: He had wavy blond hair that looked scraggly almost. And he had large shoulders and a thin waist and short legs.

S: Was he there when you blew everything up?

J: He was; he was one of the first to die.

S: What was his life like?

J: It was an unfulfilled life for him. He had spent his life taking orders from a very evil dictator and doing very terrible things to people with the promise that one day he would do things right when he had the chance. He thought that one day he would correct the wrongs that he was forced to administer, and as time grew, he learned of my powers and he thought that one day when I was ready to hand them over that he would be the one responsible for this victory.

S: He knew of your powers?

J: The old leader had told him about me. The old leader did not feel that he would live to see me hand off the powers, so the new leader had been groomed for this.

S: Tell me more about the actual explosion.

J: I was given the red crystal and held it to my chest. I can still remember that it was the last thing I felt before I felt my body rip into two. There was a very specific type of meditation that I understood to do. It allowed me to go through my mind into this other world and pull open the door that I saw in front of me. The energy that they had horribly extracted from all those Animal People was done by using our red crystal and because of that, it had created a worm hole. They had not figured out how to send the Animal People through this wormhole that they had generated. And it was through this wormhole that I could go.

S: Why did the Atlanteans want this wormhole created?

J: They did not know what it was. They were just trying to create experiments to understand our crystals better. The wormhole that they opened is how I was able to connect to the energies, and from this wormhole I could send these energies back into the energy system that they had there in Atlantis. It sends the energy back into Atlantis where it creates almost a shock wave, and I was able to crack the whole island open through explosions. And in this meditation it looked like a leaking door that I had seen as a child, and I was able to pull this door open, and this time instead of water, it was a very hot bright light. It was more than hot; it was a laser that shoots out horizontally around me.

S: How did you know that the wormhole was created?

J: This is what I see looking at it from above. I didn't know this at the time. This is on closer inspection that it appears that this is how it worked.

S: Did you have to do anything else to get these crystals to misfire?

J: It was like they were waiting for me to just pull the trigger. I did not have to line anything up or create an intention for it. It was ready for me.

S: So, all you had to do was hold the crystals while you just open the door in your meditation?

J: It looks as if I was just a vessel my entire life for the plans that were to occur. There was so much that had been planned beforehand that had to be executed perfectly. It took a lot of orchestration beyond me.

S: Can you tell me more about this explosion?

J: It was very natural. The whole process felt like I'd known what to do and it had been programmed into me. It was surprising how I did not have to do much in order for it to occur.

S: What did the explosion look like from above?

J: It looks at first like a terrific light that just shoots out everywhere. As I look at it from this perspective, I see that it creates a radius of light around me and within just a moment, the light causes everything to collapse around itself and shoot up into the sky. It just begins to disintegrate and fry everything around us.

S: You said earlier that the laser cut you. Anything else you notice from this new perspective?

J: It cut me in half... I felt it cut across me... but that was the last thing I felt. For others, I see that it was very tumultuous. The island exploded and underground it caused these explosions to carry through in the rocks underneath, and then the explosions started happening all over Atlantis, the island itself. It takes a whole day, but through the day it just crumbles and falls into the ocean in different places. There was this steam that started piling out from these big holes that were opening up, and this steam is very hot. It is burning everything around it, and then the earthquakes begin. The Earth is just cracking and cracking all over the place. And there are many... it is not instant for everyone... there are many who are traumatized greatly for having to live during that day, and then to die at the end during the final explosion.

S: There was a final explosion?

J: Yes, the final explosion happened right as the sun was setting, and submerged the few who lived into darkness. It just looks like everything falls in, and then once it's covered by water, it looks like a long incision where everything is rushing into it. Then it goes the opposite way, and everything just blows into the sky and goes everywhere. The light itself felt like a force that cuts right into you, and it was so white, so bright.

S: Did you feel the explosion?

J: I did, for just a second. I felt it cut right into me.

S: Did it feel painful?

J: For just a second, but I didn't suffer. I felt the first imprint of it. It was something I wanted to feel. It wasn't something I was hiding or scared of.

S: Where did it cut you?

J: Underneath my chest, through my body. So, the red crystal that I placed on my chest must have been at that level. I don't think I was very tall either. Probably under 5'5".

S: Were you shorter than your captors?

J: Yes, they were taller than me; there was a lankiness to them.

S: Tell me more about how you preformed the explosion?

J: There was information and power that I had been hiding within me. I had hidden it away in my DNA, my memory, and in my blood for years and years. I had more of it in me...some of it I gave away to the young girl to be saved, but enough was left inside of me so should they bring me to the right place in the right time, I would be able to malfunction, what we would call a nuclear reactor. But it was a different type of energy that I can't understand, it was powerful. It was what powered the entire civilization.

*S: **So, all this time you were the vessel to destroy Atlantis**?*

J: Yes, it was not the intention of myself to do that, but it was the purpose of my existence.

S: Could you tell me more about that?

J: It was the purpose of my existence to reset the experiment. When great injustice arises, they call on certain people who have been here a very long time to step in and to help reset the operation, to bring it back to a homeostasis, so that we may begin again and try once again to perfect the evolution that we are trying to achieve.

S: So, you were always the vessel?

J: It just looks so impersonal as I look at it from this perspective. It was less my choices in that life and more my choices before it. But not just mine; this was important for many.

S: Would it have been possible for this not to have happened?

J: There were a few instances where I was given the opportunity to abandon my position, but I did not take them.

S: Before you entered that lifetime, did you know that this was how it would end?

J: Yes, I volunteered to reset that civilization. I knew that it was necessary in ways that are good for our development.

S: Why is this good for our development?

J: We were progressing in ways that were not working toward the goal that had been our destiny. This is something that has happened many times before. They (the watchers on the other side) have stepped in when they needed to intervene and would send someone who had been here for a long time to help reset.

S: Why someone who has been here for a long time?

J: Because they understand the inner workings of people, and they are able to absorb the trauma of these lifetimes better than those who are new to this planet.

S: How did you absorb the trauma of that lifetime?

J: It was very deep, and they had to put me to sleep for quite a while after that lifetime. It was deeper than they thought it was going to be.

S: Has all of that trauma been absorbed?

J: The trauma is seen differently now as we recount this story... seen for what it was, an organized and predestined, and necessary experience.

S: Were there any survivors?

J: Some. Before this explosion happened, they had the inclination to leave. They began their journey away.

S: *I've heard that most of them went to Egypt. Is that true?*

J: Most did. The ones who went to Egypt were the most successful, but there were others who went to the central east coast of America...it looked different there then. Some went to the northern coast of America. Some went to central Europe...the rest seemed to just die off after some time.

S: *Are there any remnants of Atlantis?*

J: Some start up civilizations in the Northeast corner of the United States and have left some remnants that do not fit in.

S: *What do these remnants look like?*

J: Stone carvings, things carved into stone that don't add up to the things that historians are studying. But there are so few of these remnants now, it looks like there will be more unearthed in the future that will be of a huge assistance in understanding these people. There is a type of X that they used to describe Atlantis, like a pictograph, a symbol that they carried on. It will predate many things that people will believe that it could be from.

S: *Can you see this X in your mind right now?*

J: Yes.

S: *Open your eyes. Can you draw it?*

I put a paper in front of Jen, and this is the drawing:

S: This symbol will be unearthed someday?

J: Someday it will be found on rocks that archaeologists will uncover.

S: What does that symbol mean?

J: It was the ancient symbol for the island of Atlantis.

S: Will anything happen when this is uncovered?

J: It will begin to allow the connections with the other records that the people have found and will place this back to that time, to show this time existed, and that these predate the civilizations that we are aware of.

S: Is there anything else about this symbol that looks interesting or important?

J: The X is to symbolize that all experiments have a beginning and an end, and it is a reminder when we see this to use our time wisely on this Earth. The little loop is the jumping point that we must create during our time, the jumping point out of this X into the unknown.

THE SYMBOL OF AMUN/ LYMURIA

S: Did your island of Amun have a symbol as well?

J: Yes.

S: Could you draw that for me now?

I put the same paper in front of Jen, and she drew this symbol:

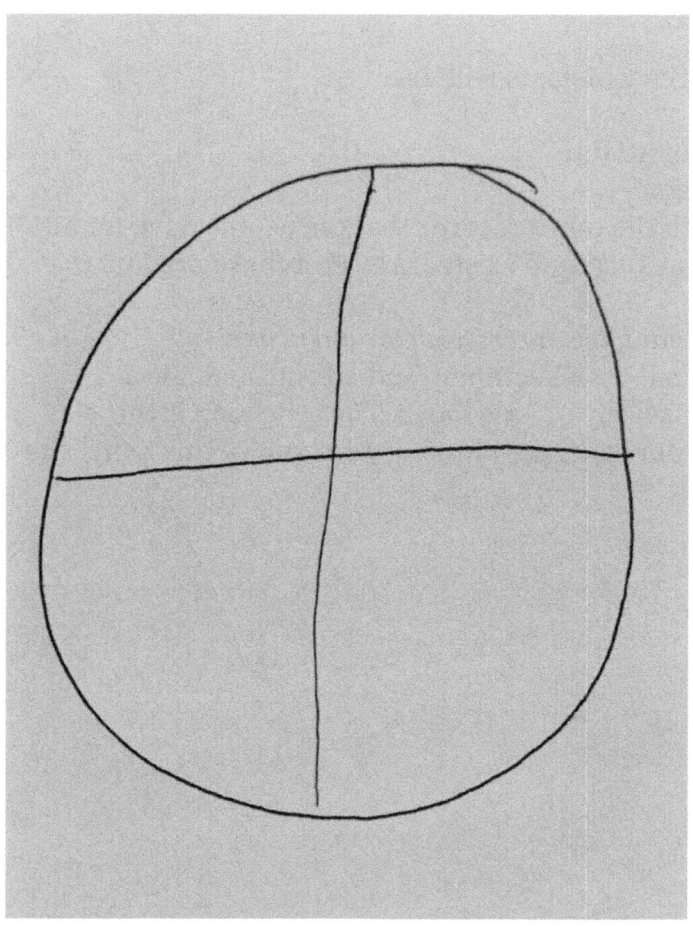

S: What does this symbol mean?
J: It is the symbol of our island.
S: Will this ever be uncovered as well?
J: It will be remembered within the minds of all who have seen it.
S: There is a place in Bimini under the water off the coast called the Bimini road, and it looks like cobblestones under the water. Many believe it was part of Atlantis. Was it?
J: This came after Atlantis, but it predates many of the civilizations that they believe could have been responsible. It was built in the aftermath of Atlantis, within 5,000 years of the destruction of it. This was created on the banks of sand that were accumulated after the explosion of the facility that housed the Animal People. People were drawn to that area because of the strange energy that was still being emitted from the water. They thought it was a God of the Sea, and these people built these roads there. They were even able to tap into some of the ideas from Atlantis, and that is where they came up with the ideas to create these roads and these advanced versions of their society. They were influenced by the energy without realizing it.

S: What happened to all the information that the young girl carried and everything that you transferred to her?

J: It got weaker and weaker over the years, and now people who still carry it, don't realize they carry it.

S: How would someone know if they carry this?

J: They might feel that they have a different ability, a different insight into things. It's weaker but it's still something that has difference to it.

S: Tell me more.

J: There is more to our past lives than we are told. This information does interact with our genetic codes as well, which are in there for a reason. There is a very special link between who you come back as and who you were, as well as who your ancestors were.

S: Do you get a sense as to why that is important?

J: It is important in that it is a choice that you can make to see things through to the end.

S: Tell me more.

J: It seems like some people, who are just visitors to this planet, it doesn't affect. But the people who have been here since the beginning and who are here to see this experiment through to the end, have a connection in the DNA that keeps them within the same genetic line of ancestors. It seems like there is trauma in DNA that you can work out.

S: Why is that important?

J: Because it looks like there are some things that are too big to finish in one life, so they are expanded over several generations in order for specific things to be fulfilled. For example, there are many who are waiting for this information to come back to the surface.

CHAPTER 23: THE AFTERMATH

My curiosity naturally led me to ask about the aftermath of the great cataclysms my clients presented in their sessions. How could humanity have continued after such great upheaval? Were there any survivors who could trace their lineage back to these lost civilizations? I wondered what were the lessons that were to be learned from these traumatic events. Jen was shown an interesting perspective of the aftermath of the Atlantis explosion.

S: Let's drift and float to right after you have left that life as a prisoner in Atlantis where you can view that entire life and see all of the details. What do you notice?
J: I was put to sleep for a very long time.
S: Tell me about that process. Was this right after you left your body?
J: This was right after I felt the light cut me in half, but before I felt any pain, any true pain. I felt this immense freedom and happiness suddenly, then all of a sudden, I felt like I was encapsulated by something, like a concrete womb around me.
S: How did that make you feel?
J: I felt very sedated and very tight.
S: Was it a good feeling, or no?
J: It wasn't bad, but I wouldn't say it was good either.
S: What was the purpose for this?
J: The Watchers on the other side needed me to hibernate. The life that I had just left was too traumatic and I needed to rest.
S: How was this rest process; how did you go about resting?
J: I don't remember much during the rest process, but I know I was gone for a while.
S: About how long do you think?
J: A couple of thousand years.
S: As you were resting, did you have awareness?
J: Light awareness, but I think the minute they realized that I had that awareness I went down again.
S: How did you come out of this?
J: I was told I was ready to begin reviewing; I was told I had rested enough.
S: When you were resting, were you able to recover?
J: I felt there was a tremendous amount of anger and grief and trauma that was so deep inside my body that the rest was needed.
S: Did they go about removing this?
J: No, I just had to be rested in order to understand what had happened and what was going on in order to prepare myself for the next existence. And because so much time had passed, the review took a very long time as well.
S: Could you tell me about this review?
J: When they take you out of the encapsulation, it's almost as if you sit down with a group of... they're not people, they're not angels, they're something in between. They have a very beautiful presence to them, a very beautiful glow, they don't have the same needs as

humans. They can float; they can telepathically communicate instantly. They're not harmful; they're very generous and good. They're very knowledgeable, like omnipotent in their knowledge, and they want you to start at the beginning and they go over your entire life with you.

S: How does that feel?

J: It feels necessary at that point because you're rested and now you can look at it in a different way. You can look at it from the outside in, which helps you process rather than from the inside out.

S: How did you feel looking at this life review?

J: I had tried once before, and I wasn't ready, so they put me back to rest. The second time I was ready. It took a very long time because I had a very long life and there was a lot to understand there.

S: A long life in years?

J: Yes, in years. I was eighty-eight when I left. I had grey in my hair and wrinkles.

S: What happened after your review? Could you tell me more?

J: It was a feeling of freedom. It feels like I am floating above a map. I can see what looks like the world, but it looks more like a map than it does terrain.

S: Tell me more.

J: I'm just floating above everything and it seems more like a globe. I'm looking at how different it looks. That is what is interesting about it. How the shape of everything has changed so much.

S: Tell me more about that.

J: It's interesting that it is very easy to get from place to place here; you can transport yourself very quickly. You can go from one place on this map to another place very fast.

S: When you look at that globe, can you see where Atlantis was?

J: Yes, it looks like there is a dark blue giant crater under the ocean, a giant hole that is filled with mud and debris. And there is even more mud piled on top that comes in through the middle of the current. There is mud everywhere. It makes boat passage go a different route. People have to go North in order to pass it.

S: There are people around there?

J: People returned back a long time later, as populations begin to grow again, and they start to explore once again.

S: What did Atlantis look like right after it was destroyed?

J: The mud is the most noticeable thing you see from the top. It looks like embankments of mud all throughout the ocean in that area around this big blue crater. It looks like the mud is going to the East of the crater and piling up closer to Europe.

S: Is there any water on top of the mud, or just mud?

J: During the tides it changes because it looks like the water can go up higher above the mud, and it looks like it can strand ships. It looks like it strands many ships in it. It could also be visible and avoidable. A very skilled sailor needs to learn their way around it in order to pass safely through it.

*S: Could you tell me about **the Bermuda Triangle**? Is that not where Atlantis was?*

J: It is a remnant of the red crystals that are still underneath the water there. They are in a few different spots, and that is where you get the triangular shape in that area.

S: Where did these red crystals come from that make up the Bermuda Triangle?

J: There were three different collections that I can see. I can see the crystal that was responsible for the destruction of Atlantis, but I'm not sure where the other two collections were from.

S: So, the red crystals are responsible for the strange occurrences over the Bermuda Triangle?

J: Yes, as well as the many ancient devices that are still under the water there. They still create a negative magnetic pull that can make things go haywire in that area. Every now and then the crystals can create a perfect storm that can activate and open up a different realm that people can pass into.

S: Where do the people go if they pass into this other realm?

J: It looks like it is an identical realm to this one, a parallel realm.

S: What's different about this realm?

J: It's an alternate version of your life, of everyone's life.

S: When you pass into that realm, do you realize it right away?

J: Yes, you can feel it. You know it is not your place, and unfortunately you cannot go back.

S: Are there many different realms?

J: There are, but you are only focused on one. These other lives in other realms are extensions of you living out different aspects of this existence to get the full experience. The existence that you are in is just one facet of many that you created.

S: Is there anything else that seems interesting about the Bermuda Triangle?

J: No, now I'm looking at where my palace in Amun used to be.

S: Tell me more; what do you see?

J: Many times in my dreams I've gone there. There is a house that's built on the blue-green water. The water runs though there, and it is very clear and shallow. The water comes up to about my knees. There is no one around; this is where the palace used to be, the island. It looks like it is just sand and water now.

S: Tell me more.

J: There were huts built there on top of poles. It feels very comforting to be there, very peaceful. It doesn't feel harsh or sad, just feels like I'm home.

S: When did you go visit this place?

J: I'm remembering the first time I went to visit. It was a few years ago in this life.

S: How did you visit that place?

J: I had opened up enough of the memory to visit it in my sleep. I wanted to see what was left of it.

S: Who built a hut there?

J: Some descendants of the people who were left stranded after the Island sank. There were some people who left Lymuria alive who wished they were dead. They had to eat bodies to survive; they did not want to, but had to. There was nothing but darkness because of the ash and soot all around them. There was no food or clean water either.

S: What did they do to survive?

J: Terrible things. Some had to drink the blood of others to survive.

S: Where did the survivors stay?

J: They originally stayed on the tops of the rocks that emerged from the water. It was rocky terrain at first, then when the seas returned back to a normal color, they learned to push these long bamboo poles into the sand and begin to build bamboo huts on the top of them. Any kind of driftwood that would pass through they would take advantage of, and they would begin to build up off the water and on top of the water so that they were close to a food source. They had to live through very terrible times themselves.

S: *Tell me more about that?*

J: I realize now that I wasn't the only one that was going through a living hell.

S: *How does that make you feel?*

J: Mixed, because I don't want the company of that feeling, and to know others had to suffer. I feel like I need to fix that for them, that my suffering wasn't enough.

S: *Is there any way to fix that?*

J: No, because it's been over with for so many thousands of years and there is no way to directly fix that.

S: *Tell me more about those people who you see there. Were they able to restart a civilization?*

J: They did, and they were able to build a lot of colonies and travel between many islands. These island civilizations would rise up and fall many times. They would fight cousin to cousin not realizing that where they came from was originally the same place.

S: *Why would they fight?*

J: Over resources. And the world became a very male dominated place after these cataclysms happened.

S: *Why?*

J: The memory of the female leadership was too much. They were blamed for a lot of what happened, and it repressed the female leadership back.

S: *Why were they blamed?*

J: They're just synonymous with the downfall of this great civilization, and it creates an inequality for women because of this. There is a curse associated with our names.

S: *Why?*

J: With our failure to continue our destiny, our legacy amongst the people of our land.

S: *Are those huts built over where Lymuria used to be?*

J: Yes, but it seems like there are many, many layers of white sand and sediment that covers it.

S: *Are there any remains?*

J: Yes, but very, very deep underneath the ocean and earth are the crushed remains of certain rock and stone structures. Most of the other stuff had disintegrated and corroded and had transformed under so much pressure that it's unrecognizable. Whatever bits and pieces of things that were not destroyed are mistaken for other groups of people in the South Pacific, the island that has the large statues of the men looking outwards, Easter Island. Those statues are from our island. There are also deep wells that people step down into and big faces carved into rock that are half cracked under the water. These are of our faces too.

S: *Is your face on one of the rocks?*

J: Yes, but it's cracked into many pieces, but it is still there. They emerge from time to time when the water's flow changes. It will emerge and it will submerge again, like a legend for people to see as they come out of the water.

S: When you visit where the palace used to be, what do you do there?

J: I had only gone there one time before to visit that I can remember. And I went and just put my feet in the water. **I never thought I would get the chance to remember this and to complete it like this. And to feel this water in this place again on my feet is just a very complete feeling.**

S: Tell me more?

J: It was in a dream that allowed me to transport myself into this location. This was before we started pulling this information. I didn't understand while it was happening, I just appreciated the feeling of completeness, but I understand now what that was as I look back at it.

S: Is there anything else interesting or important about what you are looking at now?

J: No, just that this is the completion of that life and the beginning of something new.

S: You said before that there are many trapped souls. Could you tell me more about this?

J: There are many, many of them. They're not trapped there; their **souls are trapped in a specific way that there is a trauma in their DNA and that is where they are stuck**. That is where the soul is stuck. The DNA carries this trauma within it, and it is very deeply, deeply imbedded into people now. There are a lot of people now who are not understanding what is bothering them.

S: They don't have any way of knowing?

J: Some have a feeling, some have had the ability of breaking through and understanding it, but many are still stuck and unaware. They don't even have a remote idea that this is an issue in their lives.

S: What is the best way for a person to become aware if they are stuck like this?

J: There are so many ways for each individual, but the best way to look at it is that it will happen for each person in the time that they have chosen in their pre-existence. And they will always be given chances again in this life to open this up and address this.

S: They are?

J: Yes, the opportunity will always be provided for them. If they decide that this isn't the life that they would like to work this out in, then they can continue to carry this trauma with them and work it out in the next life.

S: What about the majority of the people alive now? Are a lot of people choosing to work this trauma out in this particular lifetime?

J: Yes, it looks like it was a very big orchestrated effort once again to try to shift... **a great shift happens when a large group of people settle a karmic debt.**

S: Tell me more about that.

J: There is a large shift in the way we move forward as a result, and people become different, and it could have good effects in that way.

S: So, people will become different?

J: They can complete this and once they do, they can move forward into something different upon this completion that would propel them into different places, paradigms, and different parallels.

S: Do you mean that that is one of the reasons why there is a shift going on right now as mass amounts of people are settling a karmic debt?

J: Yes, that is definitely one of the reasons. Settling this karmic debt unlocks your ability to travel to other planets. You can choose for your next existence to be somewhere new, as you have finished this cycle through releasing this trauma from your soul.

S: I'm curious about the parallels to the virus in our reality now and the virus in Atlantis. Could you tell me more about that?

J: There are many parallels, especially in the beginning phases with the panic and stocking up, avoiding people, as well as the isolation. The difference is the dictatorship that takes over as an afterwards result in Atlantis.

S: Is this why there are so many worried about that happening now, since it happened then?

J: Yes, **many are triggered as they see the similar things, but we are choosing differently, we are choosing love.**

S: Why do some people choose to leave from this virus, to pass from it?

J: It looks like it is just the end of their mission. The end of their road; it is what has been organized by them in their pre-existence. They are also the ones ascending now.

S: Is it ever an accident to pass from this virus?

J: No, there aren't any accidents within this; this is very well orchestrated and very well planned. All that are here on the planet now sought their opportunity and understand their ends.

During a different session, Mary had come to me seeking information about Atlantis, as she had always felt a pull towards the mystery surrounding its destruction. As I gradually led her into a hypnotic state, I found she had travelled not to a past life, but to the so-called "Akashic Records," a metaphysical destination believed to hold the history of all universal events. This is a short segment of Mary's session:

S: What do you become aware of?

M: I am looking at the Akashic Records; I'm asking if I can open the records on Atlantis?

S: As you look at those records, do you get a sense if there is a reason why people say Atlantis will rise again?

M: It's figurative. The pillars of Atlantis are very similar to the pillars of our current society, especially our technology and innovation and our very masculine driven society. The tenants are the same, so in a sense it is currently rising.

S: In the records was there ever a virus?

J: There were many viruses and diseases during the time of Atlantis because they were doing things that they shouldn't have, and that was the catalyst for their ultimate destruction.

S: Why did it lead to their destruction? Tell me more.

M: Their experiments and what you would call a vaccine changed the human DNA. This ultimately led to their destruction.

S: *How was Atlantis destroyed?*

M: I'm looking... there was a great cataclysm. It looks like floods and earthquakes; the destruction looks intentional. It had to be done, but I cannot see who decided this.

S: *Are many people reincarnated from the time of Atlantis?*

M: Yes, many souls that have lived in Atlantis are here now to release this trauma and choose to do things differently.

S: *Are there any similarities of the current time we are living in now and the times of Atlantis before its destruction?*

M: Definitely the Zeitgeist, the desire for more and more and more, the collective masculine energy of pushing, striving and being the best with no regard for the feminine aspect that is in everything and in each human. This is very similar to the state of the world currently.

S: *If you scan the records of Atlantis, do you see the lessons?*

M: Yes, the lessons of that time are very important. The lesson from Atlantis was to not forgo the other side, that you need the yin and the yang to have a complete society. You can't have the innovations without the compassion, or the masculine energy without the feminine. A balance is always needed.

S: *So that was the lesson of Atlantis? What was the lesson of Lymuria?*

M: The lesson of Lymuria was that you cannot be apathetic in your level of surrender. There is a time to stand up, to fight, to be counted, to make a claim for what you know is right. You cannot always be in 100% receptivity. You can honor the feminine, but that is not the only place to live. You need balance, and both of those societies lacked balance and polarity. Lymuria was a continent of beautiful people with open loving hearts. There are many of them back here and living again. You see them; they are people with open, bleeding hearts. They are idealists and sometimes they do not see the bigger picture, and they have blinders on. These are the people we ask to wake up, stand up because they have the power to be spiritual warriors. They have the power to create a world that is balanced. The teachings live in their hearts, and they are a part of this planet and a part of the awakening.

S: *Could you tell me more?*

M: Yes, the teachings of Lymuria are in part what humans are here to understand about their power and their purpose. They are to love one another, to be compassionate, to speak to one another heart to heart. And to know that no human is greater than another. Those are all Lymurian teachings. They are available to everyone.

S: *Is there anything else that looks interesting or important as you look at these records?*

M: Yes, it is important to tell you that I see you there. You had one lifetime in particular where it looks like you went to the Sphynx! It looks like you made that trip more than once and took notes and recorded many things about that experience. You put them in a book; I can't see the book, but it is a published book. It has a cover on it, but the words are in hieroglyphics. All of your findings are in that book. Over the years the information was changed, and I need to tell you that it looks like that is one of the reasons why you're back in this life. You are here to bring that lost information back and publish it in a new book.

S: *Do you get a sense of what information I found then?*

M: I can't tell for sure, but it looks like records of lost information.

When Mary was saying these things I almost fell out of my chair. Mary did not know at that time that I was compiling this book, and this was very confirming information as I'd heard this once before during a session with Jen. I was delighted to see that they had more information regarding this.

M: There is another message; there is something they would like to tell you.

S: *Tell me more. Who are they?*

M: A group of light beings. They wish to speak.

S: *Go ahead. What would they like to say?*

M: There is information; Mary is a portal.

S: What is this information?

M: Truth, light, empowerment. There is strength in words; there is strength in the message that is coming. That is, to be aware is important, but to be awake is of upmost importance. There is much fear and control at play and has been at play for thousands of years. The old control is dying and those who control are panicking. It is almost time for the big shift. Humans are learning that even if the world were to be that of control and chaos, no one truly controls the mind, the heart. It's the physical aspect, which is fleeting, that they wish to control. The shift is… what the controllers don't understand… is the more real that they see this world, the less real that the real world is. Past the veil is where the truth is. There are entities and energy that are of divine source that are guiding, that are wielding the path. That is real, but those who cannot sense or see it, fear it. That light is coming, in whatever form. You can call it the Holy Ghost, the light above your head, the light in your heart, the awareness. There is a shift that is coming and will happen within everyone, that is Truth. I can encase you in a box, in a cell, and unless you give in to the darkness, you would still be free. There is a truth in knowing that all things come from light, come from source, and that is where you do not return, **you never left**. That awareness is not understood by the masses, so the so-called controllers of your world see the here and now, but when they shift and transition, they realize that they just played a role. Their role is of saying "Look I'm in control over you, you will do as I say." Wait, the waters of Lymuria are coming and the destruction of Atlantis is coming, the destructive force does not care that you claim power over the masses. The veil of truth passes through all whether you accept it, acknowledge it... it becomes you. It is in your essence. It is not even important to understand that the veil of truth is passed; you know it on some level. There is not fear in the here and now; that's make believe. The magic is when you sense that all that is around you is imagined, and that these worlds are created for these experiences, created for the sharing, the knowing. For when you return, then all is known. And so it is.

CHAPTER 24: THE CAT PEOPLE OF ATLANTIS- A TRIBUTE TO DOLORES CANNON

With such prevalence of cat symbols in our ancient history, I felt an unsettling need to find out if any of the Animal People who showed feline characteristics had survived, or perhaps even thrived in a world free of Atlantean rule. I knew I was not the only one who felt a connection to this subject. Dolores Cannon, QHHT originator, wrote of her quest to solve the mystery of the Cat People in her book "The Convoluted Universe, Volume 2." In an early chapter, Dolores shared an interesting regression where her client found herself in ancient times and believed she was part feline and held immense powers of alien origin. Despite the research Dolores performed after the regression, she could find no other information to help her piece together the connections she saw. On page 63 of her text, she says: "I also had no luck in finding any mention of "the Cat People," except that it was known that cats were highly respected and worshiped in Egypt. So, I decided to go ahead with this book even though I do not like to leave loose ends. Maybe someone out there has the answers and can share them with me."

Unfortunately, Dolores Cannon passed away in 2014 and was unable to find the connection before her unexpected departure. Throughout writing this book I have felt Dolores pushing me from the other side to uncover our lost history. I know she works behind the scenes to help me get this information out to you. This is what I found while picking up where Dolores left off looking further into the plight of the Cat People during a session with Jen in the summer of 2020.

S: Could you tell me about the Cat People of Atlantis?
J: There were people who had children affected by the vaccine side effects that they kept hidden away; there were families with several children who had cat features to them. They lived on the far outskirts of Atlantis, on the corner that would be closest by boat to this huge sand bar that would stick out of the ocean. Once you arrived onto this sandbar, you could continue on it and it would bring you to the Sphynx.
S: There was a sandbar that would bring you to the Sphynx?
J: It looks like it, yes, a huge sandbar, and right before the end of Atlantis this family is terrified that their children would be taken from them, so they sneak the children out of Atlantis right before the cataclysm happened.
S: Did they know about the cataclysm?
J: No, it was a family with a bunch of Cat Children; there were five or six of them. They were terrified of the police of Atlantis storming into their home and ripping the children away. They did not know that the cataclysm was about to occur. They were only acting out of the fear that their children would be taken from them. They took not only their own children, but they took other people's Cat Children as well for safe keeping, and they left on a boat in the middle of the night with all of these children.

S: Tell me more.

J: They were scared, wet; it looked like a very wet ride.

S: What did these Cat Children look like?

J: They were all very different looking. Most of them had the eyes that were very distinctive, a cat shaped eye. A lot of them were very thin and lithe. They had the temperament of cats and they also had a very aloof way of being about them. Some of them did have fur, but it wasn't a fur that covered their entire body. It was more on the arms, legs and chest where it just looks like the genetics were confused and weren't sure what was what there. But there was no one with whiskers or a tail; some of their nails would come in a bit more like claws with a bit more of a padding under the feet and hands to allow them to have a bit more maneuverability. It was mostly the mental powers that they possessed that set them apart.

S: Could you tell me more about the mental powers that they had?

J: The Cat People were able to focus very, very closely on certain things. They were able to then levitate objects because of this. They would stare, and stare, and stare and finally the object would begin to shake, and it could move upward. And some of them became really good at controlling this; but others were not.

S: So, it wasn't a definite?

J: No, but that ability was something they saw quite a bit of. The other ability they had was tapping into this invisible channel of energy that was around the world, the ancient lay lines. They could tap in and they could pull out ancient information, and that was another reason why they were aloof. They understood more than the rest of us about our origins and all that was created around us because they could tap into this.

S: So those were the children that were born after their parents took the vaccine or after the experiments?

J: This was at the end of Atlantis. These Cat Children were the result of parents who had received the vaccine and who had been hidden at birth. None of them understood their true power because the true power comes from using the precious gems, the precious metals as a conductor. So, they only ever saw things that would confuse them or were minute in comparison to the powers they would have possessed had they been exposed to things like the red crystals, silvers or gold or coppers. Even aluminum was very useful too.

S: Did they know they had these powers?

J: They knew that they were different, but they didn't understand the full extent of their powers because many were not ever introduced to these stones or metal.

S: Did the government know about their powers?

J: Yes, not at first, but over the many years they grew in their understanding as they experimented on those mutated humans that they captured.

S: So, the police were banging down the doors to try and get any of these Cat Children?

J: Yes, and they would pay off people. Often it would be their neighbors who they would pay to rat them out, to expose them.

S: *And they would take these children and use them to extract their energy, correct?*

J: Yes, and to experiment on them and ultimately remove the life from them. They were disposable batteries.

S: *So, they were on the boat? Where did they go?*

J: It was a rough, wet ride. They were all completely on edge, very alert, scared. And they land on this sand bar. The boat literally embeds into the sandbar, and there is a storm beginning all around them, so they begin to walk the sandbar as the waves are crashing up around them. And it goes on for quite a while. They walk for a little more than a day and the water does recede down, and the sun is out, and they see the Sphynx in the distance, only it has the face of a jungle cat. They can feel the power coming from within it. They are drawn to it. They know there is something there. And they go and camp underneath it, and they are also exposed in their dreams to the energy that is held within. Instead of leaving, they stay, and they begin a community as they aren't alone there. There are others already there and they are very welcoming.

I was surprised to hear that there were others already there, and they were very welcoming and not looking to create enemies with the new arrivals. Jen described a small colony that had been set up by the descendants of those who escaped the great wave of Lymuria many generations before. It was a deep thought to hold that the survivors of both cataclysms had found their way to each other, and now could find a way to live happily ever after. I asked Jen's subconscious to tell me more.

S: *Why are they so welcoming?*

J: They are not looking to create enemies. They were very happy in their new colony, and they remembered their own forceful expulsion from their homeland of Lymuria, and the tales that had been told. They welcomed people because they were the descendants of the survivors of Lymuria, and they had begun a new colony close to this very sacred land. They began to work together, and the Cat Children could begin to unlock the mysteries that were hidden in the Sphynx, in the stone. The Cat people learned that they were able to channel using gold, and the people who had come already from Lymuria had this gold that they had discovered and mined from the earth. The Cat Children instinctively made these circular devices that they would place on their heads. With these devices they would put their head up against the Sphynx close to the paw, and they would download the information, and ask it questions that would help to create this new community again. Using the ancient power, they could create a flourishing community for the descendants of both islands of Lymuria and Atlantis to restart.

S: What happened to that power?

J: It was eventually misused and taken over.

S: How?

J: There was a heavy domination of a male energy that came in and it changes the way the people are treated, the way they feel, the energy that they emit, and how they can connect to these things. It went from being something very pure with that eternal celestial love that they received into something that is very coveted and dangerous. It becomes dark and it ultimately destroys the people there as well.

S: What happened?

J: The information and power becomes too mixed. The original point of it was lost and it becomes like a cult where there are very bad intentions to control people using this information. And it creates a wealthier upper echelon with plenty of people to control and have power over them because of this.

S: Where was this?

J: Egypt.

S: How did this happen? How did someone start to control the people?

J: Someone said that it was the divine right of theirs to reclaim this energy, to harness this energy. And they enslaved people to build things to create it and to harness it. And they held them under the guise that this would be the beginning of a new way that would be beneficial for all. But it wasn't; it was just a way to get them under their control.

S: What happened to these people?

J: There is a very long history there, but eventually the ultimate end of it was when they replaced one cult for another, and it continues to be passed from cult to cult and eventually it is forgotten, and that is the end of the old world and the beginning of this world.

S: When you go to Egypt now, are there any remnants of the old world?

J: None that are visible; they are stuck underneath the sands there, but some will be discovered. There will be a very large windstorm sometime in the future that will uncover things that people haven't seen for...it looks like almost fifteen to twenty thousand years.

S: What type of things?

J: The other Sphynx will be uncovered; there is another one.

S: What does it look like?

J: Shattered, the face has been shattered down; you will only see the body.

S: What does the face look like?

J: It did have the face of a lioness at first; it is the female counterpart to the male. But this was built later. It was not built at the same time as the original Sphynx.

S: Was this built during Atlantis, or no?

J: The original Sphynx was built by earlier, other worldly colonizers that came to Atlantis.

They came with their technology and used it to build that. They may have had some help from the humans, most of it was done using their technology though. During the escape and the regrowth after Atlantis, the second one was built with the guidance of the Cat People using these gold bands around their heads. They were guided to build it.

S: *Who told them to build this?*

J: They received messages from within the Sphynx, files that have been filed away in there on how to build it. They felt it was a celebration to build it, like a stepping-stone for them and something they needed to do. And they built it very quickly out of enthusiasm. It serves as something that they build things all around. They do not build around the original Sphynx because they felt that it is sacred. But the new Sphynx is more of a socialization place, a place to meet, a place to congregate, share, worship and a place for offerings. They would place oils and flowers and things before it; it was theirs.

S: *How was it destroyed?*

J: It was destroyed at the onset of the change that occurred after the beginning of the new treatment of women. Women became less powerful and more closed up, shrouded almost and as that began to shift, this destruction was symbolic of that change.

S: *How did this happen?*

J: It was a power seize. The female Cat People who had escaped were better at conducting this electricity and retrieving this information than the males who were brought over. It wasn't indicative that the men were less powerful in conducting this electricity, it was just in this specific case that these males were not as good. But what this allowed for was for those young women to create a very powerful community around this female centered power that they derived directly from the Sphynx. And it takes a few generations, but eventually there is one man who rises up against them to claim the power for himself. And it becomes a very violent time. It is the beginning of a very, very violent time.

S: *Could you tell me more about it?*

J: People were very happy and peaceful in their homes for quite a long time. They lived in these stone huts that were filled with what looks like mud on the sides of the walls to fill in the cracks in the stones, and it keeps them cool. It was a very peaceful and happy place. And this man begins to put ideas into the other men's heads. At first it comes off as crazy and everyone just begins to ignore him, but eventually, it causes this big divide within their society.

S: *Why?*

J: Because many people believed they should not be ignoring this man, that instead they really should be helping him. By ignoring him it had only created a stronger power behind him, and other people were attracted to what he had to say and started to follow him. Once he had a small group of like-minded men behind him, this energy begins to take over them.

The energy grows and it grows with this anger. They are angry and do not feel that they are important to their society and this makes them angry. This man got as many men to turn against the Cat Women and their female society as he could because this man and his followers wanted that power and energy. They weren't exactly sure where the power and energy was coming from, but this man just said all of the right things to have people question these Cat People, and to disbelieve them.

S: *What happens next?*

J: A huge massacre, things were set on fire, ransacked. People were killed in their homes; their children killed in front of them.

S: *Were these Cat Children or regular children?*

J: Both, and there were fires that were set that lasted for days with smoke coming out of these stone buildings.

S: *Is this man in our history anywhere?*

J: No.

S: *Why the fires and killing? What did he want to accomplish?*

J: They wanted the control and power of everything and that is exactly what they got because by the time this is over the majority of the people that were Cat People or who sided with the Cat People were dead, and it begins the new era of the Egyptian Empire.

S: *Were there any Cat People who survived or were they all killed?*

J: There were others who survived who went to other places, but the ones from ancient Egypt were killed.

S: *Are there any descendants of Cat People today?*

J: There are very few, but there are many who relate because they were these Cat People in their previous existences.

S: *Are there any physical features that you can see today that come from these Cat People?*

J: Yes, the eye shape is a very recessive gene. They would have a very large almond shaped eye, ones that have a slight slant upwards to it.

S: *Anything else that seems interesting or looks important about what you are looking at right now?*

J: Just a lot of things on fire. The smoke came out of those stone buildings even days after. The power made the control-hungry men lose their minds, and that is the problem. The truth was distorted because they tried to use this power for their own benefit and not the benefit of all.

S: *So how did this take away the power of women?*

J: It scared women from wanting anything that would put them in a position of power because the female Cat People were the most powerful people in that society. That was the beginning of the loss of power for women. After these two great cataclysms there was a feeling that women were responsible for the downfalls of those civilizations. And it wasn't a feeling of " I heard this and it must be a fact," it was something in the background quietly simmering in people's subconscious as a result of this.

CHAPTER 25: THE ABORIGIONES, AND OTHER SURVIVORS

Those who survived the turbulent times of Lymuria and Atlantis seemed to have been spread out throughout the world. I looked to find out more information from Jen during another session that could help shed some light on the path they took.

S: We know that after the cataclysms some survivors went to California and Egypt. Were there some survivors who went to other places as well?

J: Yes, there were many who went to different smaller communities along coastlines. They worked their way inwards and connected back with each other. These were the beginnings of the societies known as our ancient societies. But the small community of the survivors that went to Northern America, high up past Nova Scotia, in that area, did not survive. With climate change, they froze; they could not keep up with the cold that descended too quickly. The same thing happened to the survivors who went to Northern Europe at the time. However, there was a group of survivors who went to Australia. The Aborigines in Australia are true descendants of Lymuria.

S: Tell me more about them?

J: They still hold many cave systems in Australia that are off limits to others. The caves go deep red tunnels throughout rock that is made of petrified trees. Within these natural tunnels they would keep their ancient records that account the tale of the destruction of their earliest people, the islanders of Lymuria.

S: What do these records say?

J: They tell the tale of the visitors, the Atlanteans, and how they came and ended up destroying their homeland. There are also records of how some of them survived and made their way to what is called Australia now. But these records are so old and misunderstood that they have new meanings to them now.

S: Do the Aborigines in Australia look like Lymurians did?

J: They have many, many characteristics that follow in suite, though time has changed certain features.

S: What did it change?

J: Time has changed the face slightly; their face used to be rounder, but they still have the same skin and hair color, and the body shapes are still the same.

S: What about their philosophies?

J: Some philosophies have fallen through the cracks of time, but others have remained, such as their connectivity to energy, to an otherworldly spirit, and understanding of their true origins coming from another world. These all remain the same. But they have had many trials and tribulations through the course of the centuries that have passed where they have had to go against what they originally believed in order to survive. And they migrated away from many of their societal patterns.

S: *What about their walkabouts? Was that practiced in Lymuria?*

J: No, that was a result of them having to prove themselves many, many generations later down after the wave. It was a way to show the continuation of the human spirit's survival after it leaves the body, and of continuing to test and to deal with the circumstances around us.

S: *If you scan all the survivors and descendants of Lymuria, which group of people alive today most resembles them?*

J: The Aborigines of Australia, and those who populate several of the islands around the Pacific. The Samoans would also bear a very close resemblance. There is generally a rounder face with dark brown reddish skin and curly dark hair. The Lymurians were strong, stout and a smaller type of person. And for some, they still carry on the silver streak in their hair that many in Lymuria did as well back then.

Below is a short segment with a client under hypnosis exploring what it was like for her to survive the cataclysm in Atlantis. Many clients have recounted similar tales of survival, each unique in their own perspective. This is Anne's story:

Anne: I had a strong sense that something was wrong, but I didn't share that with anyone.

S: *Tell me more about that.*

A: I need to get my bearings, but I feel as if I'm on a boat and something terrible just happened. I had a sense that something was about to happen, but I did not want to be ridiculed or worse. No one speaks out around here. But I had a strong sense that things just weren't right; things just weren't adding up.

S: *Tell me more about this place you just left?*

A: There is a lot of dark technology here. There is a lot of manipulating energy, manipulating people, playing God. It seems they have many people enslaved here as well.

S: *Tell me more about that?*

A: Some of the slaves look slightly animalistic, but they seem to be slaves who spend their lifetime focusing this energy. It's like a large beam of light that they are projecting, like a laser.

S: *What was your life like there?*

A: It was all I knew. Lots of innovations, technology and work.

S: *Tell me more about what you're doing now?*

A: (Started to cry) I realize that the place I'm talking about was destroyed and that is why I'm on this boat. There is nothing left of where I just left.

S: *How do you feel?*

A: Scared, devastated, not really sure of what will happen.

S: *Are you alone or by yourself?*

A: No, I'm with someone. They also had a feeling and we both took as many artifacts and information that we could save. But the weight and pressure of not being able to save all and not being able to save everyone is very heavy on my heart.

S: What happened next?

A: We finally arrive at another place where we see people. They look scared to see us at first, then realize that we're harmless at the moment, scared and hungry. So, they let us stay. I believe this is where Egypt is now.

In my experience so far, I have come across many who have explored and released this same type of trauma from that lifetime in Atlantis. There are many people who recall harrowing journeys of survival amongst the horrible destructions. Many have carried the survivor's guilt they developed from their past into future lifetimes. Additionally, I find it interesting that a common thread these clients have all shared is that they are claiming to rebuild in this life what was once lost to them long ago during the great cataclysms.

CHAPTER 26: THE DIVINE FEMININE REAMERGING

The concept of women being the cause of our Earthly problems has often been presented in the ancient story of Adam and Eve, in which a woman questions authority, seeks knowledge, and is ultimately punished along with humankind as a result. I do not think it is a coincidence that nearly all religions and ancient cultures find themselves attached to this ancient misinformation. In my work it has become apparent that in the aftermath of the cataclysms of Amun and Atlantis, women have become the scapegoat for the deep trauma we undertook as a collective society. The events of their time were so unsettling that it entirely altered the balance of masculine and feminine, and ushered in a path of subjugation for women that still exists today. In this subjugation, there is much of us that we blindly look to change for reasons we cannot understand. With this in mind, I wondered about Jen and her initial quest from our earliest hypnosis session in which she strived to lose weight. I found it odd that throughout the whole process of gathering our information for this book, Jen had never lost the weight that she had once claimed was her biggest issue. I wanted to know why.

S: When Jen first came to me, she wanted to lose weight, but why hasn't she? Did she not release all that she needed to? Are we missing something?

J: The point of her body being put into this lifetime and experiencing these things was never to lose the weight. The point was to embrace the human body, and to love the human body that she was given, a body that she in fact chose. This is not about the weight. The weight was a delivery mechanism. It was not part of her; it was part of her purpose here. It brought her to the places that she needed to go. Now the fear of the weight is gone; the pain of the weight is gone. The stigma of the weight is gone; it does not feel like it is something that is foreign to her anymore. It feels part of the body now and comfortable in the body.

S: What happens to Jen now that she has accepted this weight?

J: It is a relief of anxiety and the self-image that losing the weight would have never solved. Losing the weight would have put her back into this situation in the next lifetime. This is part of something much bigger.

S: What?

J: This is part of the awakening. This is part of people needing to see their bodies as the vessels they really are, and to shed one's self from how their body looks, and to appreciate the body, to not change the body for others. It is all clearly outlined in the history of your life. It is in the history of where you have shied and hidden away from your truth and it is time to begin to open those doors. This is about the Divine Feminine re-emerging and claiming its rightful place.

It is important to note that the re-emergence of the Divine Feminine is not a solitary path. The reclamation of this divine energy of self-love has its balance in the rebirth of the Divine Masculine. A male client came to me during the summer of 2020 looking for direction in his life, as he felt stuck and could not understand why. He felt he didn't know what his purpose in life was, yet he had a very strong feeling that he had a big purpose. He knew a QHHT session would help him find the answers that he needed. This was the surprising answer his Higher Self gave him when asked what his purpose was.

S: What is Ed's purpose in this life?

E: He is here for great things, very important things. He is here to awaken the Divine Feminine in others, to help the Divine Feminine reclaim its rightful power.

S: Tell me more about this?

E: The Divine Feminine is an energy that has been with us since the beginning of time. There has always been a masculine and feminine side, a duality needed to achieve our highest potential. The Divine Feminine represents the feminine connection to ourselves, our intuition, compassion and creation that is within all of us. Unfortunately, it has been squashed under thousands of years of lies, torture and deceit. It has been squashed, dethroned, and shamed. The true beauty has been taken away under lies of what beauty should look like. The Divine Feminine has never been about one size or one look. The Divine Feminine is the ultimate creator of many different sizes and different ideals of beauty. **The time for the Divine Feminine to resurface is now. His purpose in this lifetime is to help bring this back.**

S: How does he go about doing this?

E: His job will be to create art, sculptures of the true bodies of women that will, when seen by others, create a pathway in their minds that will remind them of their own true beauty. When men or women see these sculptures, they will see them and understand that they should look at their own bodies as beautiful no matter what size and shape. It is in his true gift to this world the seeds will be planted to create great change.

S: Does he understand his purpose now?

E: He does. He is feeling a sense of surprise, however, the truth of this feels to him like something he has always known.

CHAPTER 27: MOVING FORWARD

In my last session with Jen, she felt a loving presence around her. The beings or energy called themselves the Gate Keepers, and when we asked to speak with this presence, this is what they had to say:

J: There is something pushing down on me right now, like a force, an energy.

S: *Why is something pushing down on you?*

J: Something is trying to communicate with me.

S: *What do they want to say?*

J: There is a group of individuals, they don't look like humans but more like spirits, almost like a wisp of energy and they are in the formation of a triangle with one in the center and several to each side almost like in a size order.

S: *What do they say, and why are they here right now?*

J: They say that they are the ones who have been giving us this information. This information must not sit, this information has been released for this reason. They say to share this information with as many as we can. The world is ready for this now.

S: *Why is this information important for people to know now?*

J: Because we are about to create a massive shift. We are so close to achieving the next level that we have been striving for, too much is hindering upon our development. The breakthroughs that we will make in the next few generations because of what we are changing now will have an unparalleled impact on our society to where we will wonder how we lived before we understood ourselves in this way.

S: *What breakthroughs are we making?*

J: Humans are beginning to open their minds and see themselves clearly and understand that they are not just simply products of their imagined society around them, and that each person is not created based off of other's opinions. Humans are starting to understand that they all have deep origins, deep opinions, and deep reasons for being here. There is a need to understand this now.

S: *What will occur as a result of understanding this?*

J: This new shift into a different mentality, a new way of being with each other and a new way of understanding oneself. It will rekindle an understanding within the mind. That is the purpose of your stories, to bring back the original understanding of who we are and why we are here, and to allow that thought to innovate our next level, our next platform that humans will grow into.

S: *Are we on the right path as a human collective?*

J: Yes, however, there is always uncertainty and that is one of the reasons this information needs to be shared, as this knowledge will help all to understand their mission on this planet during this time. There has been a great misleading of our people and the majority of us do not understand who we are and why we are here, and that is the main purpose of this.

S: Who are we, and why are we here?

J: We are an ancient grouping of beings who have come from different planets and have continuously moved from planet to planet in order to see what the next and the next will be, to continuously evolve and to spread throughout the Universe, so that we may never be alone.

S: Why hasn't this information been available before?

J: There have been too many disasters that have upset this information stream, too many reasons to control people that have also upset this information, and the information has become too mismatched and jumbled to really pull it back to its original truth and its center. We have been led astray from it, and it has been a detriment to our society, but we are ready for this information to be released now.

S: Who am I talking to?

J: They say that they are the Gate Keepers, that they are allowing us to do this.

S: Who are these Gate Keepers? Can you tell me more about them?

J: (Laughs) They say they are us, that we are the physical manifestation of them.

S: Do they say anything else?

J: They say this information has been released, and now is the time to share all of this information with the world.

Final thoughts:

I feel now more than ever that this alternative understanding of our origin is needed in our society and must be brought to light. I feel this story is important not only because of the strong parallels I see around us to our ancient beginning, but also as a warning that we should not go blindly into our future without considering the powerful darkness of the past. This darkness has influenced our opinions of what we believe to be valuable and has given us a false impression of our own worth. This darkness has molded us to be distrustful of each other and has divided us so that we stay stagnant and feed its misery. It is through understanding this darkness that we can finally shed its influence and merge into the light. And, in that way, create a new world of love, equality, and balance. As I put the final pages together for this book, I cannot help but reflect on the journey Jen and I have taken. I originally set out to help Jen regain her health and continued with the desire to help her free her story. But as I reflect, I see she is not alone in her transformation. I too have changed immensely, and I see now that this journey was not one that Jen was meant to take alone. This journey was for both of us...and, indeed, for all of us.

ABOUT THE AUTHOR

Sarah Breskman Cosme is a Certified Master Hypnotherapist and a Level 3 QHHT practitioner living in the Florida Keys. To contact her visit www.theholistichypnotist.com

Made in United States
North Haven, CT
08 January 2022